# DETERMINANTS OF SUCCESS IN UN PEACEKEEPING OPERATIONS

Jacques L. Koko
and
Essoh J. M. C. Essis

University Press of America,® Inc.
Lanham · Boulder · New York · Toronto · Plymouth, UK

**Copyright © 2012 by**
**University Press of America,® Inc.**
4501 Forbes Boulevard
Suite 200
Lanham, Maryland 20706
UPA Acquisitions Department (301) 459-3366

10 Thornbury Road
Plymouth PL6 7PP
United Kingdom

Library of Congress Control Number: 2012932326
ISBN: 978-0-7618-5865-2 (paperback : alk. paper)
eISBN: 978-0-7618-5866-9

The views expressed herein are those of the authors
and do not necessarily reflect the views of the United Nations.

♁™ The paper used in this publication meets the minimum
requirements of American National Standard for Information
Sciences—Permanence of Paper for Printed Library Materials,
ANSI Z39.48-1992

To:
Barbara, my queen of peace;
Julie, my princess of peace;
Jacques Jr., my little angel of peace!
For your love and sacrifice!
　　Jacques L. Koko


To my father, my mother, my six brothers and sisters, Marie-Therese,
Hillary Jo-Ann; and to every other person who taught me to choose, love and
live "peace".
　　Essoh J.M.C. Essis

# Contents

# List of Tables and Figure

# List of Acronyms

| | |
|---|---|
| CONDUR | Conflict Duration |
| CONIS | Conflict Issue |
| CONTYPE | Conflict Type |
| DOMREP | Mission of the Representative of the SG in the Dominican Republic |
| DPKO | Department of Peacekeeping Operations |
| FLEC | Front for the Liberation of the Enclave of Cabinda |
| IFOR | Implementation Force |
| INTERFET | International Force in East Timor |
| ISAF | International Security Assistance in Afghanistan |
| MINUGUA | United Nations Verification Mission in Guatemala |
| MINURCA | United Nations Mission in the Central African Republic |
| MIPONUH | UN Civilian Police Mission in Haiti |
| MONUA | United Nations Observer Mission in Angola |
| MPLA | Movement for the Liberation of Angola |
| NUCIST | Number of Civilian Staff |
| NUCOCO | Total Number of Countries Contributing Military and Police |
| NUMIPO | Total Number of Military and Police Personnel Deployed |
| ONUB | United Nations Operation in Burundi |
| ONUC | United Nations Operations in the Congo |
| ONUCA | United Nations Observer Group in Central America |
| ONUMOZ | United Nations Operation in Mozambique |
| ONUSAL | United Nations Observer Mission in El Salvador |
| PEGREP | Percentage of Great Power Involvement |
| PKERA | Era of Peacekeeping Operation |
| PKO | Peacekeeping Operations |
| PKODUR | Duration of Peacekeeping Operation |
| PKOMAN | Mandate of Peacekeeping Operation |
| PKORE | Region of Deployment of Peacekeeping Operation |
| PKOTIME | Time between the Start to Conflict and the Start of PKO |
| PKOUT | Peacekeeping Outcome |
| PRIO | Peace Research Institute of Oslo |
| SFOR | Stabilization Force |
| SWAPO | South West Africa People's Organization |
| TONUFA | Total Number of Fatalities in Conflict |
| TOSPEND | Total Spending |
| UN | United Nations |

| UNAMIC | United Nations Advance Mission in Cambodia |
| UNAMIR | United Nations Assistance Mission for Rwanda |
| UNAMSIL | United Nations Mission in Sierra Leone |
| UNASOG | United Nations Aouzou Strip Observer Group |
| UNAVEM I | United Nations Angola Verification Mission I |
| UNAVEM II | United Nations Angola Verification Mission II |
| UNAVEM III | United Nations Angola Verification Mission III |
| UNCRO | United Nations Confidence Restoration Operation in Croatia |
| UNDPKO | United Nations Department of Peacekeeping Operations |
| UNEF I | First United Nations Emergency Force |
| UNEF II | Second United Nations Emergency Force |
| UNGOMAP | United Nations Good Offices Mission in Afghanistan and Pakistan |
| UNIIMOG | United Nations Iran-Iraq Military Observer Group |
| UNIKOM | United Nations Iraq-Kuwait Observation Mission |
| UNIPOM | United Nations India-Pakistan Observation Mission |
| UNMIBH | United Nations Mission in Bosnia and Herzegovina |
| UNMIH | United Nations Mission in Haiti |
| UNMISET | United Nations Mission of Support in East Timor |
| UNMOP | United Nations Mission of Observers in Prevlaka |
| UNMOT | United Nations Mission of Observers in Tajikistan |
| UNOGIL | United Nations Observation Group in Lebanon |
| UNOMIL | United Nations Observer Mission in Liberia |
| UNOMSIL | United Nations Observer Mission in Sierra Leone |
| UNOMUR | United Nations Observer Mission in Uganda-Rwanda |
| UNOSOM I | United Nations Operation in Somalia I |
| UNOSOM II | United Nations Operation in Somalia II |
| UNPKO | United Nations Peacekeeping Operations |
| UNPREDEP | United Nations Preventive Deployment Force |
| UNPROFOR | United Nations Protection Force |
| UNPSG | United Nations Civilian Police Support Group |
| UNSC | United Nations Security Council |
| UNSF | United Nations Security Force in West New Guinea |
| UNSMIH | United Nations Support Mission in Haiti |
| UNTAC | United Nations Transitional Authority in Cambodia |
| UNTAES | United Nations Transitional Administration for Eastern Slavonia, Baranja and Western Sirmium |
| UNTAET | United Nations Transitional Administration in East Timor |
| UNTAG | United Nations Transition Assistance Group |
| UNTMIH | United Nations Transition Mission in Haiti |
| UNYOM | United Nations Yemen Observation Mission |

# Preface

This book is a revised version of Jacques Koko's dissertation, submitted to the Graduate School of Humanities and Social Sciences at Nova Southeastern University in Florida on July 9, 2008. It presents an empirical assessment of United Nations peacekeeping operations (UNPKOs), in an effort to identify the major variables or factors that determine the success or failure of such operations. The decision to study the determinants of success in UNPKOs emerges out of our shared concern about the widespread belief that UN peacekeeping operations are often not successful, as well as from our desire to inform scholars, practitioners and the general public about the conditions in which they can be made more successful.

Our study uses data from the UN Department of Peacekeeping Operations' website and other relevant sources to compile an original dataset on 15 variables representing the most important characteristics of 46 peacekeeping operations carried out by the United Nations Organization between 1956 and 2006. A relatively well-known statistical technique named "principal components factor analysis" is then used to exploit the correlations between the 14 independent variables in order to regroup them into a smaller set of factors that can explain the success or failure of these operations. The four factors identified by our factor analysis model account for more than 70% of the variance among the characteristics of the 46 peacekeeping operations.

These results show that the success of a UN peacekeeping operation can be explained by a small number of factors that are related to four categories of variables, namely: i) the *scope of resources invested in peacekeeping*; ii) the *duration and intensity of conflict and time of preparation for peacekeeping intervention*; iii) the *political support for peacekeeping from the UN Security Council*; and iv) the *type of conflict*.

We hope that the results of this study will be helpful to UN policy-makers, peacekeeping scholars, and to all the practitioners involved in the design, planning, implementation, and evaluation of UNPKOs. We also hope that this book will be a useful learning tool for students and researchers in the fields of political science, conflict analysis and resolution, and international peace and security studies.

Jacques Koko and Essoh Essis
Union, New Jersey
December 2009

# Acknowledgments

Completion of this research project and publication of its results would have been impossible without a significant amount of support from several institutions, as well as guidance and assistance from many generous colleagues, friends, and relatives.[i]

We are especially grateful to the leadership of the Department of Conflict Analysis and Resolution and of the Graduate School of Humanities and Social Sciences, Nova Southeastern University, for encouraging and supporting this research. We are also grateful to the United Nations Department of Peacekeeping Operations for allowing access to critical data on past UNPKOs.

We want to express our admiration and appreciation to Dr. Judith McKay and to Dr. Cécile Mouly for making helpful suggestions on research methodology, concept clarification and operationalization, as well as on ways to refine significant parts of this work. We also want to thank all the other colleagues who have assisted us on this project and whose names are not mentioned here; as well as all our students, around the world, from whom we have learned tremendously.

Finally, we must acknowledge and thank our parents and our families, for the many sacrifices they have accepted, and for their unwavering moral support.

**Endnote**

1. We would like to express respect and gratitude to all of them by humbly acknowledging them here. Pretending to mention all those generous men and women here would be too ambitious because such endeavors would require a tremendous investment in the task of remembering and naming a multitude of people of goodwill. We only mentioned here a few people whose generosity, cooperation, and sacrifice enabled or allowed us to come out with the final outcome of this project.

# Introduction

*Peacekeeping* is one of the three major concepts developed or endorsed by the United Nations Organization (hereinafter referred to as "the UN") to identify and distinguish the various types and cases of civilian and military intervention conducted under its mandate to promote global peace and security through the prevention, management, resolution, and positive transformation of intrastate and interstate conflicts. The other two concepts are *peacemaking* and *peacebuilding*. Johan Galtung believes that these concepts are important because they carry three different approaches to peace. In his view, peacekeeping is necessary to stop or reduce violence through the interposition of military forces between the conflicting parties while peacemaking promotes political reconciliation through mediation, negotiation, arbitration and conciliation; and peacebuilding works to achieve peaceful change through structural means such as socio-economic reconstruction (Galtung 1975).

Former UN Secretary-General Boutros-Ghali has provided standard definitions for each of these concepts. Peacemaking falls under Chapter VI of the United Nations Charter, which prescribes the "pacific settlement of disputes" (Boutros-Ghali 1995, pp. 45-46; United Nations 2005, p.24). It involves political negotiations and mediations by diplomats and officials as well as arbitration and judicial settlement to address and resolve conflict issues. Peacebuilding refers to a broad plan of actions to transform post-conflict or conflict-torn societies into stable countries that enjoy sustainable peace. Peacebuilding strategies include state rebuilding, local capacity-building, confidence building, negotiation, mediation, facilitation, trauma healing, restorative justice and practices fostering forgiveness and reconciliation, among others (Boutros-Ghali 1995; Lederach 1997; Zehr 1993; Sampson 1997, Schirch 2005). Even though the UN Charter does not specifically mention the concept, peacekeeping falls under its Chapter VII, which authorizes the deployment of international troops to maintain peace and security. Peacekeeping refers to the various activities carried out by civilian and military personnel positioned in war-torn states by the UN and related regional organizations, with the consent of conflicting parties, to monitor ceasefire or to handle post-settlement reconstruction (Boutros-Ghali 1995; Zartman 1997).

In other words, UN peacekeeping designates a complex set of policies, programs, projects, and actions in conflict prevention, management and resolution carried out by the UN, on behalf of the international community, through the deployment of UN troops, police officers and civilian personnel in conflict-shattered countries or regions (Boutros-Ghali 1995; Diehl, Druckman, and Wall 1998; Miall, Ramsbotham and Woodhouse 1999; Berman and Sams 2002; Wall, Druckman and Diehl 2002; MacQueen 2002; United Nations DPKO 2003; Durch 2004; Greig and Diehl 2005; Bellamy, Williams, and Griffin 2005).

Our interest in the study of the determinants of success in UN peacekeeping operations (hereinafter referred to as "UNPKOs") was spurred by a number of important observations that might be categorized as practical, theoretical, and methodological considerations.[1] At the practical level, we note the fact that peacekeeping operations have become the standard strategic option and method utilized by the UN for the management of intrastate and interstate conflicts, especially after the end of the Cold War. The first UNPKO was launched in 1948, under the name of *United Nations Truce Supervision Organization (UNTSO)*, and the UN has initiated sixty-three (63) peacekeeping operations between 1948 and 2008. 75% of these operations have been initiated since 1988 (Greig and Diehl 2005). In fact, the growing number of UNPKOs initiatives in the early 1990s has led to the creation of the United Nations Department of Peacekeeping Operations (DPKO) in 1992 to plan, manage, and implement peacekeeping operations adequately.[ii]

In addition, we understand that peacekeeping operations do consume considerable amounts of human and financial resources that could be put to alternative good uses. As of February 2007, the total deployment of UNPKO personnel since 1948 had reached 101,642, including 73,307 military, 9,444 police officers and 18,891 civilian staff members; and the total number of fatalities in peacekeeping operations had reached 2,337 deaths (UNDPO 2007). As of September 2007, the total count of UN personnel serving in peacekeeping operations worldwide was 82,541 uniformed personnel (including 70,396 troops, 9,617 police and 2,528 military observers), 4,857 international civilian personnel, 11,443 local civilian personnel, and 1,986 UN volunteers; that is, a total number of 100,595 personnel serving in 17 peacekeeping operations (UNDPO Website 2008). According to a report by *Peace Dividend Trust* and the UN Peacekeeping Best Practices Unit, the United Nations spends approximately US$ 5 billion a year for peacekeeping missions (Carnahan, Durch, and Gilmore 2006). The figures provided by the UNDPO are even higher, with the field expenditures for 2006 approximating US$ 6.03 billion; the estimated cost of peacekeeping operations from July 1, 2007 to June 30, 2008 being about US$ 7 billion; and the estimated total cost of UNPKOs from 1948 to June 30, 2008 about US$ 47.19 billion (UNDPO 2007; UN Website 2008).

Finally, we are aware that Africa has hosted the largest number of all UNPKOs, including 17 (almost 37%) of the 46 operations scrutinized in this study. It currently hosts 6 (33%) of the 18 UNPKOs still on-going in the world (Liberia, Sudan, Côte-d'Ivoire, Democratic Republic of Congo, Ethiopia-Eritrea, and Western Sahara), and about 70% of the total number of "peacekeepers" deployed worldwide (UN Department of Peacekeeping Operations 2007). The financial cost of these operations is also considerable. The United Nations Department of Public Information reveals that UNPKOs in Africa have cost just under US$ 3 billion for the year 2004 alone, and that the approved budget for 2004-2005 was US$2.80 billion (United Nations Department of Public Information 2004). In 2005, there were 15,000 peacekeepers in Liberia, at a cost of US$ 750 million a year (BBC News online 2005). However, despite the efforts implied by these numbers, peace still remains fragile or inexistent in the host countries, spurring the contention that UNPKOs do not matter because most of them are unsuccessful, or even ineffective (Greig and Diehl 2005).

On the theoretical level, we note that as a consequence of the generalization of the use of (and reliance on) UNPKOs, there has been a significant increase in the number of studies that examine the conditions and motivations for their creation; describe their structure, resources, actions and modes of operation/implementation; assess their outcomes, effects and impacts; and/or seek to identify the determinants of successful peacekeeping operations. As expected, with the development of the literature on peacekeeping operations comes the habitual conflict of views and conclusions regarding their nature and modalities (typologies), their philosophical and moral justifications, the best way(s) (methods) to study them, and especially the proper criteria for assessing their processes and outcomes.[iii]

The prevailing belief is that UNPKOs are generally not successful. In addition, we tend to be dissatisfied with the fact that scholars came up with relatively long lists of conditions for successful peacekeeping.

Urquhart (1987 & 1990) suggests nine conditions for successful peacekeeping: i) *broad support (political, military, diplomatic and financial)* for the operation; ii) *feasibility of the mission mandate*; iii) *viability of the political context*; iv) *composition of the "force"*; v) *collaboration from the disputing parties*; vi) *quality in the command process*; vii) *skill and sensitivity in directing the force*; viii) *discipline of the troops*; and ix) *lack of external imposed-upon solution.*

In the same vein, Evans (1993) identifies seven conditions for the success of peacekeeping operations, namely: i) *clear and feasible goals in the mandate*; ii) *sufficient resources*; iii) *coordination between peacekeeping and peacemaking*; iv) *impartiality*; v) *local support*; vi) *external support*; and vii) a *clear exit strategy.* Both Urquhart and Evans presented interesting and useful conclusions, but they were too subjective due to the interpretative approaches that characterized their studies.

Consequently, we felt a need to provide at least a systematic summary review and a critical analysis of the major theoretical conclusions that have been proposed by scholars in this field of study and, to the extent possible, identify a small set of explanatory factors that are both empirically grounded, easily operationalizable and measurable, and most importantly, relevant for all policy design, planning, implementation, and evaluation purposes.

From a methodological point of view, we note that only a few systematic and empirical studies involving large numbers of cases of peacekeeping have been conducted. With the notable exception of a recent study by Doyle and Sambanis (2006) on UN peace operations, the few studies that provide some insights into this matter do so from a limited empirical ground, from one or few case studies *(e.g., Diehl 1994; Sambanis 1999; Urquhart 1987 & 1990; Evans 1993; Adebajo 2004).*

Diehl (1994) examined a few cases whereas Sambanis (1999) relied on the sole case of Cyprus. Adebajo's study of the factors of peacekeeping success in Africa is based on six post-Cold War case studies (Mozambique, Angola, Somalia, Rwanda, Sierra Leone and the Democratic Republic of Congo). He found that the six factors that have contributed most to UN peacekeeping success are: i) *willingness of the parties to disarm and accept the result of elections*; ii) *adoption of an effective strategy to handle spoilers*; iii) *non-existence in war areas of economic resources that aliment conflict*; iv) *cooperation of regional actors in peace processes*; v) *termination of financial and military support to local actors by external players and its replacement with external diplomatic and financial support to peace processes*; and vi) *good leadership in UN peacekeeping missions* (Adebjo 2004).

In a study of the impact of peacekeeping on peacemaking, Greig and Diehl examined interstate conflicts from 1946 to 1996 and intrastate conflicts ("civil wars") from 1946 to 1999 and found that peacekeeping inhibits negotiation and mediation efforts and decreases the probability of getting a settlement (Greig and Diehl 2005).

In their ground-breaking work on the success of UN peacebuilding, Doyle and Sambanis (2006) examined all peace processes after civil war from 1945 through the end of 1999, by comparing peace processes with UN involvement to those without it. They found that "local and international capacities" influenced positively the chances of peacebuilding success, while "hostility levels" impacted negatively the probability of success (Doyle and Sambanis 2006). It must be noted, however, that their study was concerned with peace operations in civil wars cases only and did not examine peace processes in cases of interstate conflicts. In addition, the focus of their study was to identify the determinants of success in UN peacebuilding operations by comparing peace processes where the UN was involved to those where it was not (Doyle and Sambanis 2006). As a result, their study concentrates more on peacebuilding than on UN peacekeeping in the strict sense of the concepts.

The present study focuses exclusively on UN peacekeeping operations. It builds upon the tradition of systematic comparisons over large numbers of cases in order to arrive at theoretical conclusions that are grounded in empirical reality, and are therefore operationally meaningful and policy relevant. It examines 46 UNPKOs (all UN peacekeeping operations) initiated from 1956 through 2006 to manage cases of intrastate and interstate conflicts, in an attempt to identify the most significant factors that could help to explain the success or lack of success of such operations.

Considering the surge in peacekeeping, the large size of the peace operations, and their cost, one would expect peacekeeping activities to impact the target nations with peace dividends. For a number of target nations, empirical evidence demonstrates that peacekeeping resulted in successful transitions and free elections in cases such as Sierra Leone, Liberia, and the Democratic Republic of Congo. But in other cases the rules of instability and violence still prevail as in Haiti, Sudan, and the Democratic Republic of Congo to some extent. Sierra Leone would represent a case of positive transformation because of the decrease in the level of violence following peacekeeping operations in that country, while Haiti might stand for a negative example due to continuity in violence despite the presence of peacekeepers. Overall, the context of surge in peacekeeping –with related attributes of positive or negative changes within the target nations- frames the relevance of this study.

# Research Objectives, Questions, Hypothesis and Design

Three specific research objectives are assigned to this study. The first objective is to identify the major factors that can explain the outcome of UNPKOs. The second objective is to measure the relative influence of each determinant or explanatory factor. The third objective is to arrive at empirically deduced suggestions and recommendations for future research and for policymaking.

In order to achieve the research objectives listed above, we found it necessary to ask the following research questions: Why do some UNPKOs succeed and others do not? What are the criteria that must be used in order to provide an objective measure of UNPKO success? What are the major variables or factors that can explain the variation between successful UNPKOs and unsuccessful ones? How can these variables or factors be best identified and measured?

To all these questions, we propose a simple tentative answer in the form of the following research hypothesis: The success of a UNPKO can be explained by a small number of factors that are related to four categories of variables, namely: i) the *scope of resources invested in peacekeeping*; ii) the *duration and intensity of conflict and time of preparation for peacekeeping intervention*; iii) the *political support for peacekeeping from the UN Security Council*; and iv) the *type of conflict*.

In order to test this hypothesis, we used open-source information from the UN Department of Peacekeeping Operations' website and other relevant sources to compile an original dataset on 14 variables representing the most important characteristics of 46 peacekeeping operations carried out by the UN between 1956 and 2006, a time period of fifty years. We then used a relatively well-known statistical technique named "principal components factor analysis" which exploits the correlations between these 14 variables in order to regroup them into a smaller set of factors that can explain the success or failure of these operations. The four factors identified by our factor analysis model account for more than 70% of the variance among the characteristics of the 46 peacekeeping operations.

The results from our study suggest that: i) contrary to a prevailing belief in academia as well as in the general public, UNPKOs have a relatively high rate of success (54%); ii) it is possible, and probably most effective, to identify the major determinants of UNPKO success through the use of statistical analytic models involving systematic comparisons over large numbers of cases, in order to enable empirically grounded and generalizable theoretical conclusions; iii) the success of a UNPKO is obviously a function of specific variables representing the major characteristics of the conflict and its context, but also a function of specific variables representing the major characteristics of the peacekeeping operation that is designed and implemented in order to manage that conflict.

Chapter 1 provides a systematic review of the literature that is available on the concept of peacekeeping in general and on UNPKOs specifically. In so doing, it discusses the conceptual and methodological challenges that this study faces. Chapter 2 describes the dependent and independent variables that were identified and used in this study, as well as the data sources and the techniques used to develop the dataset for statistical treatment. Chapter 3 describes the statistical methods and techniques used for data processing. Chapter 4 presents the analysis and interpretation of the statistical results. Chapter 4 also discusses the major findings from the study and their implications for theory, policymaking and research. It underlines the limitations of this study and makes suggestions and recommendations for future research.

# Endnotes

1. These lines introduce the reader to what motivates this research and to the goals of this book. They do so by stating the reasons why the authors have decided to examine the determinants of successful UN peacekeeping operations, and by describing the goals that are assigned to this research. The core rationale for studying the determinants of success in UN peacekeeping operations emerges out of the concerns expressed in the literature about the organization of the United Nations being ineffective because many of the UN peacekeeping operations proved unsuccessful (see Greig and Diehl 2005). The underlying assumption behind such concerns is that success or failure of UN peacekeeping depends solely on the United Nations. Although it can be said that the UN is responsible for the outcome of its peacekeeping operations, the analyst could also argue that the characteristics of these operations, and the characteristics of the conflict all represent critical factors that may affect peacekeeping outcome because peacekeeping is a process that evolves with specific conflict situations.

2. To illustrate how the post-Cold War era has coincided with a surge in UN peacekeeping operations, some scholars noted that the UN has launched over three-fourths of its peacekeeping operations since 1988 (Greig and Diehl 2005).

3. Despite its increased importance and the explosion of related studies, only few systematic and empirical studies involving large numbers of cases of peacekeeping have been conducted. In this regard, some of the most notable scholars include Doyle and Sambanis (2006), Greig and Diehl (2005), Diehl, Druckman, and Wall (1998), Bratt (1996), Diehl (1994). This research builds upon this tradition by making systematic comparisons over large numbers of cases in order to set empirically rooted generalizations. In doing so, the study expects to suggest the character of UN peacekeeping and some of the determinants of success in peacekeeping.

# Chapter 1

# Evolution of Peacekeeping as a Concept and of UNPKOs as an Object of Scholarly Study

This chapter retraces the evolution of peacekeeping as a concept and of UNPKOs as an object of scientific study. In so doing, it discusses the conceptual and methodological issues that have been addressed by previous scholarly works on peacekeeping in general and UNPKO success in particular, and that have motivated our study.[1] The first section looks at the history of peacekeeping activities and the evolution of the concepts developed for its analysis and evaluation. The second section highlights some theoretical perspectives on peace and conflict studies and presents the philosophical foundations of peacekeeping. The last section presents some typologies of UN peacekeeping.

## Historical Overview of Peacekeeping Concepts and Activities

The concept of peacekeeping emerged in the 1950s (Bellamy, Williams and Griffin 2004, 1). However, the practice of collective intervention for the management of international conflict can be traced back to the Roman Antiquity, where a relatively stable consensus emerged among the major powers of the Roman Empire that they shared the responsibility of maintaining global peace and security by extending law enforcement activities beyond their national borders (Bellamy, Williams and Griffin 2004). In modern times, the great powers often resorted to intervention as a way to safeguard international peace and security (Buzan and Little 2000) but efforts at multinational management of violent political conflict were formalized in the 19th century with the creation of the Concert of Europe, and institutionalized in the 20th century, through the League of Nations.

### The Concert of Europe

The *Concert of Europe* was created in 1815 when the major European powers agreed that the preservation of international peace and security in the post-Napoleonic era required not only widespread diplomatic cooperation among themselves but also the systematic use of collective interventions to successfully manage international conflicts (Mangone 1954; Ikenberry 2001). Thus, several peacekeeping operations were organized in the 1820s under the auspices of the Concert of Europe, including the Austrian expedition in Naples and multinational interventions against Barbary pirates and against Turco-

Egyptian forces during the Greek War of Independence (Bellamy, Williams and Griffin 2004).[ii]

However, that commitment to collective action for international peace and security did not last because the *Concert of Europe* collapsed under the combined effects of a clash of narrowly defined national interest ambitions and of the internal revolutions of 1830 and 1848. At some point, "preserving the peace was synonymous with securing the interests of the great powers" (Kissinger 1994; Bellamy, Williams and Griffin 2004, p. 60).

## The League of Nations

The *League of Nations* was created in 1919 to safeguard international peace and provide collective security in the aftermath of World War I. Articles 11.1 and 16.2 of the *Covenant of the League of Nations* outline the agenda of the organization to prevent and respond to international conflict through peacekeeping-type activities for collective security. Article 11.1 states that:

> Any war or threat of war, whether immediately affecting any of the Members of the League or not, is hereby declared a matter of concern to the whole League, and the League shall take any action that may be deemed wise and effectual to safeguard the peace of nations.

Article 16.2 is more specific:

> It shall be the duty of the Council in such cases to recommend . . . what effective military, naval or air force the Members of the League shall severally contribute to the armed forces to be used to protect the covenants of the League.

In conformity with its Covenant, the League of Nations undertook several international peacekeeping and mediation activities between 1920 and 1925, including during the Aaland Island dispute between Sweden and Finland (1920), the Albanian territory dispute between Greece, Yugoslavia and Italy (1921-1923), and border clashes of 1925 between Greece and Bulgaria (Barros 1970, p.87-126; James 1990, p. 40-42; Bellamy, Williams and Griffin 2004, p.69).

In 1920, the *League of Nations* authorized the deployment of an international force of 3,300 troops made of British, Italian, Swedish, and Dutch soldiers to maintain law and order in Germany's Saar region, and oversaw the international administration of the coalmines of the Saar Basin. The same year, it also tried to address the dispute between Germany and Poland over the port of Danzig. Between 1920 and 1922, the League oversaw post-war plebiscites in Schleswig, the Klagenfurt Basin, Allenstein and Marienwerder, Upper Silesia and Sopron with the support of the presence of international armed forces (James 1990; Bellamy, Williams and Griffin 2004, p. 69). In each situation, the international military forces were deployed with the consent of the host territory, and they were allowed to use force only for self-defense. These two principles of consent of the parties and use of force for self-defense would tremendously influence UN peacekeeping practices in the Cold War era.

Unfortunately, the *League of Nations* would slowly give up its ambition to promote collective security and peace. By the end of the 1930s, France and Britain were actively trying to instrumentalize the League to maintain their great power status. In response Japan, Germany, the US and the Soviet Union refused to participate in the League. Kupchan and Kupchan observe that certainty, utility and inclusivity are the three major characteristics of effective collective security organizations, and that the League of Nations collapsed when it failed to display these characteristics. It did not show sufficient certainty in response to aggression in many cases; was often not able to mobilize all forms of diplomatic, moral, economic and military coercion available to its members; and tended to exclude some states from its decision-making processes (Kupchan and Kupchan 1991; Bellamy, Williams and Griffin 2004; also see Claude 1963; Bennet 1984).

When the *United Nations* succeeded the *League of Nations* at the end of World War II, it immediately sought to reinforce its peacekeeping capabilities and would soon increase its multinational intervention activities.

## UN Peacekeeping Efforts: The Cold War Years

In the Cold War era, the idea of continued reliance on the conduct of *ad hoc* multinational peacekeeping interventions came forward as a feasible alternative to that of a United Nations Army when the five permanent members of the Security Council failed to agree upon the *"Collective Security Command"* envisioned in the UN Charter. The first UNPKOs organized in conformity with the provisions of Chapter VII of the UN Charter to take actions to maintain international peace and security by using armed forces provided by members states were the *United Nations Truce Supervision Organization* (*UNTSO*, 1948-), the *United Nations Military Observer Group in India and Pakistan* (*UNMOGIP*, 1948-), and the *United Nations Emergency Force I* in the Middle East (*UNEF I*, 1956-1967). *UNEF I* would set the model for what is now referred to as "traditional peacekeeping", requiring the consent of the conflicting parties, the neutrality of the peacekeepers, and the interdiction to shoot, except in case of self-defense (Berman and Sams 2000; Durch 2004; Bellamy, Williams, and Griffin 2004).

The other UN peacekeeping efforts during the Cold War era include the *United Nations Observation Group in Lebanon* (*UNOGIL*, 1958), the *United Nations Operation in Congo* (*ONUC*, 1960-1964), the *United Nations Security Force in West New Guinea* (*UNSF*, 1962-1963), the *United Nations Yemen Observation Mission* (*UNYOM*, 1963-1964), the *United Nations Peacekeeping Force in Cyprus* (*UNFICYP*, 1964-), the *Mission of the Representative of the Secretary-General in the Dominican Republic* (*DOMREP*, 1965-1966), the *United Nations India-Pakistan Observation Mission* (*UNIPOM*, 1965-1966), the *Second United Nations Emergency Force in the Middle East* (*UNEF II*, 1973-1979), the *United Nations Disengagement Force* (*UNDOF*, 1974-), the *United Nations Interim Force in Lebanon* (*UNIFIL*, 1978-), the *United Nations Good*

*Offices Mission in Afghanistan and Pakistan* (*UNGOMAP*, 1988-1990), the *United Nations Iran-Iraq Military Observer Group* (*UNIIMOG*, 1988-1991), the *United Nations Angola Verification Mission I* (*UNAVEM I*, 1989-1991), and the *United Nations Transition Assistance Group in Namibia* (*UNTAG*, 1989-1990) (United Nations 2007). *ONUC* was the largest of all these operations, with close to 20,000 troops deployed (Bellamy, Williams, and Griffin 2004).

*Traditional peacekeeping* refers to peacekeeping as it primarily developed in the bipolar world that characterizes the cold war era. As such it aims to manage conflict between states by posting slightly armed or unarmed troops in a buffer zone between the belligerent forces in an attempt to deter them from resuming hostilities once they have agreed upon a ceasefire, and to create a space for political dialogue conducive to reaching a peace agreement between the conflicting parties. Those *peacekeepers* or *blue helmets* (so called in reference to the color of the UN stamped helmets they wear) are soldiers provided by UN member states and placed under the UN authority, at the request of the UN Security Council, to intervene in violent conflicts that threaten regional stability and international peace and security. Initially, the UN Charter did not allow peacekeepers to use force. They were simply expected to act as representatives of impartial third party actors, monitoring ceasefires and helping to create a secure haven for the diplomatic actions that are indispensable for the peaceful resolution of the conflict issues between the warring parties (Diehl, Druckman and Wall 1998; Berman and Sams 2000; Laremont 2002; United Nations DPKO 2003; Bellamy, Williams and Griffin, 2004; Greig and Diehl 2005). In short, traditional peacekeeping generally features a one-dimensional military deployment operation in support of political negotiations. After the end of the Cold War, the practice of UN peacekeeping evolved to integrate other dimensions as well.

## The post-Cold War years

In the late 1980s, the international system recorded a remarkable increase in the number of UNPKOs. "During this period the UN conducted more peacekeeping operations than it had undertaken in the previous forty years" of its existence (Bellamy, Williams, and Griffin 2004, p. 75). The increased demand for peacekeeping operations was coupled with a paradigm-level shift which led to the introduction of "qualitative and normative transformations" in traditional peacekeeping practices (Bellamy, Williams, and Griffin 2004, p.75). The qualitative transformation consists in the coupling of traditional peacekeeping operations with "the delivery of humanitarian aid, state-building programmes, local peacemaking and elements of peace enforcement" whereas the normative transformation consists in "the promotion of the Westphalian conception of liberal-democratic peace", which prioritizes the security of human beings within states (Bellamy, Williams, and Griffin 2004, p.75).

*Multidimensional peacekeeping* refers to a broader multilateral conflict intervention strategy that integrates comprehensive non-military missions and activities with traditional, military-centered peacekeeping operations. Concretely, multidimensional peacekeeping operations have explicitly and formally added strong humanitarian, economic, political, and social functions to the mostly military aspects of traditional peacekeeping operations (Abi-Saab 1992, 1995; Durch 1996; Berman and Sams 2000; United Nations DPKO 2003; Bellamy, Williams, and Griffin 2004).[iii]

Thus, while the military component remains essential in UNPKOs, the civilians elements included in multidimensional peacekeeping operations are charged with humanitarian, economic, political, and social functions in addition to their involvement in diplomatic activities such as negotiation and mediation. Besides helping the parties reach and implement peace agreements, they must provide humanitarian assistance to displaced civilian populations; assist the disarmament, demobilization and reintegration efforts; support the restoration of the rule of law; work to promote the respect of human rights in the field; assist in the establishment of transitional administrations; help strengthen public institutions; and oversee the conduct of free elections (United Nations DPKO, 2003; Durch 2004; Bellamy, Williams, Griffin 2004). After the end of the cold war, peacekeeping became explicitly multidimensional, dealing with interstate as well as intrastate conflicts.[iv]

# Theoretical Perspectives and Philosophical Foundations of Peacekeeping

The debate on peacekeeping falls within the political and legal dilemma around intervention or non-intervention to address violent conflicts that threaten regional security and international peace. In addition to legal foundations provided by Chapters I, VI and VII of the Charter of the United Nations, the intervention/non-intervention dilemma is rooted in philosophical assumptions that justify both intervention and non-intervention. Political and moral philosophy theorizes on the importance of non-intervention as it safeguards the principle of state sovereignty and citizens' self-determination (Mill 1859; Kellas 1998; Jackson 2000; Walzer 2000). However, political and moral philosophers also claim that sovereignty and self-determination could be dismissed for intervention in worst-case scenarios. They argue that intervention might be justified in the context of civil wars with cruel human suffering, in the face of severities repugnant to humanity, if there are gross violations of human rights such as ethnic cleansing (Mill 1859; Stedman 1993; Mandelbaum 1994; Walzer 2000). In other words, intervention for humanitarian purposes is ethically justifiable in the case of intolerable cruelties or massive atrocities. The justification of intervention results in making peacekeeping a third-party intervention strategy which the international community resorts to for conflict management.

The politics of peacekeeping intervention relies more or less on such philosophical assumptions, and the scholarly literature on peacekeeping follows the conflicting perspectives inherent to those assumptions.

Indeed, scholars hold divergent views on the role of peacekeeping (Bellamy, Williams and Griffin 2004), how to conceptualize peacekeeping and how to evaluate it (Druckman and Stern 1997).

Bellamy et al. (2004) argue that proponents of *Westphalian* politics and tenants of *post-Westphalian* politics strongly disagree on the role of peacekeeping in international politics. In the *Westphalian* perspective, peacekeeping is to occur and settle interstate conflict. This conception limits the role of peacekeeping to maintaining peace and order between states and supports traditional peacekeeping: here, the focus is the security of states. The post-*Westphalian* approach expands the role of peacekeeping to intrastate interventions to resolve conflict and restore peace and order. This conception of peacekeeping emphasizes the security of individuals within states and backs multidimensional peacekeeping (Bellamy, Williams and Griffin 2004). This disagreement between *Westphalian* and *post-Westphalian* perspectives echoes the "tension within the UN Charter and international law . . . as to whether the security of states or the security of human beings should be prioritized" (Bellamy, Williams and Griffin 2004, p. 2).

Some arguments emphasize the usefulness of peacekeeping, whereas others highlight its uselessness and counter-productivity (Greig and Diehl 2005). Greig and Diehl (2005) attempted to present a synthesis of arguments for and against peacekeeping.

The arguments in favor of peacekeeping are articulated around a rationale suggesting that peacekeeping could contribute to peacemaking by opening a space for dialogue between the disputants (Greig and Diehl 2005). Peacekeeping can also open a space for other crucial peacebuilding activities such as the conduct of peaceful elections and institution-building (Bellamy, Williams, and Griffin 2004). By helping to maintain a ceasefire, for example, peacekeepers can provide a space for conflicting parties to engage in peace negotiations. In this regard, Boutros-Ghali (1995) stressed that peacekeeping expands peacemaking possibilities. A major assumption underlying such expectation is that violent conflict discourages successful peacemaking activities (see Kressel and Pruitt 1989; Bercovitch, Anagnoson, and Wille 1991; Pruitt and Carnevale 1993; Bercovitch 1997). Further, if this expectation positively associates peacekeeping with peacemaking, it can also imply that unsuccessful peacekeeping will result in failure in peacemaking as Greig and Diehl (2005) pointed out.

A common argument against peacekeeping criticizes the fact that traditional peacekeeping does not address the root causes of conflict because it focuses solely on direct violence and not on structural violence. Other arguments negatively associate peacekeeping with peacemaking, meaning that peacekeeping limits or discourages diplomatic activities such as negotiation and mediation (Greig and Diehl 2005). This negative view on peacekeeping relies on some underlying assumptions rooted in rational choice and in Zartman's (1985,

2000) concept of hurting stalemate. Rational choice assumes that civil wars and rivalries generate information about the capabilities of conflicting parties, which help them anticipate the results of future fighting and stop the confrontations once they acquire sufficient information (Fearon 1995; Wagner 2000; Reiter 2003; Greig and Diehl 2005). According to Greig and Diehl (2005), rational choice implies that peacekeeping intervention cuts the information flow of wartime and therefore jeopardizes the end of the fighting. In other words, peacekeeping interrupts the course of getting information conducive to ending war.

Moreover, Greig and Diehl (2005) suggest that peacekeeping might decrease the possibility for the conflicting parties to reach a hurting stalemate by reducing the costs in human resources and in logistics. The notion of hurting stalemate translates a stage of deadlock where conflicting parties end up opting for negotiation or mediation after they feel that force could not help them reach their goals (Zartman 1985, 2000). The hurting stalemate reflects a state where the conflicting parties attempt to escape violence by eyeing ways of peaceful settlement (Young 1967; Holbrooke 1998; Greig 2001; Greig and Diehl 2005). In this regard, peacekeeping reduces or removes the pressure that wartime costs put on conflicting parties to opt for peacemaking (Diehl 1994; Greig and Diehl 2005).

In conclusion some proponents and opponents of peacekeeping establish a relation between peacekeeping and peacemaking. However, the relationship they observe is often limited to whether peacekeeping contributed to opening a space for diplomatic activities such as negotiation and mediation to take place successfully.

Peacekeeping could be trapped within impasses or fail if the conflicting parties experience a high level of hostility, power disparity, or relationship blockages due to previous record of enmity. Peacekeeping could also fail if the operation lacks adequate resources and support. In other words, the outcome of UN peacekeeping could be determined by a series of factors related to the characteristics of the peacekeeping operations, the nature of the conflict, and the nature of the parties and their relationship.[v]

# Peacekeeping in Relation to Conflict Management and Resolution

The international system features violent interstate and intrastate conflicts that challenge global security and peace. Conflict could be defined as a manifestation of antagonism involving divergence of interests and incompatibility of goals among parties on a social level (Mitchell 1981; Boulding 1990; Hocker and Wilmot 1991; Pruitt and Kim 2004). It is a multidimensional process that could be interpersonal, organizational, national or international (Bercovitch, Anagnoson and Willie 1991; see Hocker and Wilmot 1991).

In international politics, conflict is handled in many ways, including through negotiation and mediation. Scholars of conflict management suggest that conflict could be addressed through unilateral or bilateral strategies, or through the means of third-party intervention (Bercovitch & Houston, 1996; Bercovitch, Diehl, and Goertz 1997; Jackson 2000; also see Greig and Diehl 2005). Unilateral strategies may revolve around the use of violence for a win-lose outcome, whereas bilateral strategies involve bargaining to maximize a win-win outcome. Deterrence represents a common unilateral strategy, whereas negotiation stands for the most common bilateral strategy (see Greig and Diehl 2005, p. 623). The most common strategies of third-party intervention include mediation, arbitration, and adjudication (Carnevale and Pruitt 1992; Jackson 2000; Greig and Diehl 2005; Bercovitch, Anagnoson, and Wille 1991; Bercovitch & Houston 1996).

Peacekeeping represents a third-party intervention strategy because it involves the mediation of peacekeepers in situations of violent conflict (Wall, Druckman, and Diehl 2002). As such, the international community has increasingly been relying on peacekeeping to manage and resolve violent conflicts that trap the international system (Druckman and Stern 1997; Wall, Druckman, and Diehl 2002; Greig and Diehl 2005).

# Typologies of United Nations Peacekeeping Operations

Peacekeeping scholars have set different typologies of peacekeeping. In an attempt to understand the dynamics of UN peacekeeping, Bellamy and al. (2004) distinguish five types of peacekeeping operations, namely *traditional peacekeeping*, *wider peacekeeping*, *managing transitions*, *peace enforcement*, and *peace support operations*.

*Traditional peacekeeping* indicates the intervention of UN forces in armed conflict situations mostly between states to create or facilitate conditions that allow peacemaking through negotiation or mediation. It usually occurs after a ceasefire between the fighting forces, and implies the consent of the parties, the impartiality and minimum use force on the part of the peacekeepers (Bellamy, Williams and Griffin 2004; also see Berman and Sams, 2000). Traditional peacekeepers are tasked with patrolling buffer zones between the belligerents, monitoring borders, verifying processes of demilitarization, disarmament, and troop withdrawals. UNTSO, UNEF I, and UNFICYP represent examples of traditional peacekeeping (Bellamy, Williams and Griffin 2004).

*Managing transition* operations take place in contexts of war-shattered states' transitions from violence to stability and peace. As transitional operations, they have a clear start and end, beginning after the signature of a peace agreement and ending with the conduct of elections or the declaration of sovereignty for a new state. They are multidimensional operations because they integrate significant military and civilian components to manage a transition process and facilitate the implementation of a peace agreement. The military tasks may include patrolling of buffer zones, separation of combatants, and verification of disarmament, demobilization, and reintegration of ex-combatants. The civilian functions encompass the management of "various aspects of transition, including civil administration, policing, democratic institution-building (often including reform of the judiciary and political system) and supervision of electoral process" as well as facilitation of humanitarian aid and promotion of human rights (Bellamy et al. 2004, p. 112). "Managing transition" operations are based on the consent of the former conflicting parties; they are impartial and make minimum use of force. Examples of "managing transition" operations include UNTAG, ONUSAL and UNAMIC (Bellamy et al. 2004).

*Wider peacekeeping* stands for the enlarged dimensions of peacekeeping operations conducted with the consent of the disputants for peace and security in an environment of "potential or actual conflict", guided by the principles of impartiality and minimum use of force (Bellamy et al. 2004, p. 128). Bellamy et al. (2005) identify wider peacekeeping with the following six major characteristics:

- *Wider peacekeeping* interventions take place during violent conflicts, either in the absence of a ceasefire, a peace agreement or in a context of fragile or collapsed peace agreement;
- They usually occur within states and not between states;
- Their military functions increase to include the monitoring of ceasefires, the enforcement of no-fly zones, the separation of troops, the disarmament of the belligerent parties, the organization and supervision of elections, the distribution of humanitarian aid, the protection of civilian staff of the UN and other NGOs, and nation-building (Berdal 1993; HMSO 1995; Doyle et al. 1997; Bellamy et al. 2005);
- They involve a high number of humanitarian NGOs that the peacekeepers need to cooperate with;
- Their mandates often change several times in the course of the operation;
- They embrace more tasks than traditional peacekeeping, but have limited resources to operate. They often lack finance and logistics (Bellamy et al. 2005).

The United Nations Protection Force in Bosnia (UNPROFOR), UNAMIR, UNOMSIL and UNAMSIL illustrate cases of wider peacekeeping (see Bellamy, Williams and Griffin 2004).

*Peace enforcement* indicates a UN or regional organizations' mandated use of military force against a state or a group threatening global peace and regional security in an attempt to "restore or maintain international peace and security; enforce sanctions; defend the personnel of peacekeeping operations; provide physical protection to civilians in conflict zones; protect humanitarian activities"

(Bellamy et al. 2004, p. 147; Goulding 1996). The concept of peace enforcement falls in the logic of collective security under Chapter VII of the UN Charter which grants the Security Council the power to identify any threat or breach of international peace and security and take enforcement measures in case peaceful means do not succeed in maintaining collective security (Boutros-Ghali 1992; Bellamy et al. 2004). To that end, the Security Council has often delegated the powers of Chapter VII to other entities, including UN member states and regional organizations to use military force on its behalf (Sarooshi 2000; Bellamy et al. 2004). Examples of peace enforcement include ONUC, UNOSOM I, UNOSOM II and UNMIH (see Bellamy, Williams and Griffin 2004).

*Peace support operations* represent multidimensional operations that combine vigorous armed force with important diplomatic and humanitarian components. They are set as impartial UN-authorized intervention of force with functions, ambitions and means to address breaches of peace and transform war-shattered nations into liberal democracies. Peace support operations facilitate the creation of an interim UN administration that works towards the establishment of a functioning state based on the rule of law and democratic principles. Their functions expand to encompass "civilian policing, institution building, infrastructure reconstruction and national reconciliation" (Bellamy et al 2005, p. 165; Holm and Eide 2000; Hansen 2000a; Mackinlay 1998). The process usually ends when the interim UN administration transfers power to a local, democratically elected leadership (Bellamy et al. 2005; Thakur and Schnabel 2001). Examples of peace-support operations include the NATO-led Implementation Force (IFOR) and Stabilization Force (SFOR) from 1995 to present days in Bosnia, the Kosovo Force from 1999 to present days in Kosovo, the International Force in East Timor (INTERFET) from 1999-2000), the International Security Assistance (ISAF) in Afghanistan from 2001 to present days (see Bellamy, Williams and Griffin 2004).

Alternative typologies of peacekeeping include the *Stimson Center*'s typology of peacekeeping and the systematic classification by Diehl, Druckman, and Wall (1998). The *Stimson Center*'s typology provides four interesting types of peacekeeping as *traditional peacekeeping, multidimensional peacekeeping, humanitarian intervention,* and *peace enforcement* (Durch 2004). However, the Stimson Center's category of *humanitarian intervention* does not seem consistent because the evolution of the practice of peacekeeping connotes all peacekeeping types with some degree of humanitarianism.

Diehl et al.'s typology classifies peacekeeping missions according to their functions, scaling different peacekeeping functions along "primary versus third-party roles and integrative versus distributive process" (Diehl, Druckman, and Wall 1998, p.33). Their classification provides twelve types of peacekeeping missions, which encompass *traditional peacekeeping, observation, collective enforcement, election supervision, humanitarian assistance during conflict, state/nation building, pacification, preventive deployment, arms control verification, protective services, intervention in support of democracy,* and *sanctions enforcement*. Even though we acknowledge and commend the merit of such a systematic classification, some of their criteria do not match the concern of our study. First, Diehl, Druckman, and Wall's taxonomy is primarily concerned "with the military aspects of peacekeeping missions and not necessarily with some increasingly civilian-based aspects of those operations" (1998, p.38), whereas our study is concerned with both military and civilian components of peacekeeping. Moreover, some of the categories seem redundant and might overlap in a given peacekeeping mission. For instance, humanitarian assistance, protective services and election supervision could well be parts of a nation-building operation because nation-building should involve a restoration of the social contract, which requires some forms of humanitarian assistance and the protection of civilians' rights. Observation could fit in traditional peacekeeping because it is hardly possible to distinguish the two types of intervention in practice (Diehl, Druckman, and Wall 1998). Diehl et al. acknowledge that their categories "are not mutually exclusive because a given military operation may include more than one of the missions outlined, either simultaneously or sequentially" (1998, p.38).

Other typologies of peacekeeping are less systematic. Prior to (and during) the Cold War, a classic typology distinguished between *traditional peacekeeping* and *observation* (UN 1991, Diehl 1994; Diehl, Druckman, and Wall 1998). During the post-Cold War period, with the increase in civil wars, and the surge in peacekeeping, the categories of *first-generation* peacekeeping versus *second-generation* peacekeeping (or *new peacekeeping*) emerged (Mackinlay and Chopra 1992; Ratner 1995, Diehl, Druckman, and Wall 1998). Ramsbotham, Miall, and Woodhouse (1999) distinguished a first generation and a second generation of UN peacekeeping from 1956 to 1995 versus a third generation of UN peacekeeping (with *new requirements*) after 1995. In the same period, few classifications considered the stage of conflict, the timing of intervention, and the function of intervention (Thurman 1992; Diehl, Druckman, and Wall 1998). Segal (1995) developed a typology following the historical phases of peacekeeping missions, taking into consideration the political conditions that authorized the missions, and not necessarily their characteristics (Diehl, Druckman, and Wall 1998). As Diehl et al. suggested those classification efforts are narrow-minded and do not make a clear distinction between peacekeeping types. They also tend to ignore the commonalities of missions (1998, p.35).

This exploratory study proposes to conduct an empirical research within a theoretical framework which suggests some factors that might affect UN peacekeeping outcome, regardless of peacekeeping typologies.

The following chapter, *Chapter 2*, describes the data sources, the dataset, and the dependent and independent variables selected for this study.

## Endnotes

1. This chapter unveils our approach to UN peacekeeping against previous scholarly works on peacekeeping. It points to the strengths and limitations of existing studies. The chapter looks at the history and nature of UN peacekeeping and the conditions for its success through a literature review that revolves around three points developed in three sections.

2. Attempts to preserve international security and peace during the nineteenth-century Europe bolstered collective action to keep *the peace*, under the auspices of the Concert of Europe.

3. The components of a multidimensional peacekeeping operation clearly integrate a series of non-military tasks into the traditional peacekeeping formula.

4. Understanding the connotations brought into peacekeeping by the evolution of the phenomenon under study is of paramount importance as we examine the determinants of success in UN peacekeeping, because the characteristics of peacekeeping are likely to influence peacekeeping outcomes. The evolution of the concept of peacekeeping shows nuances with potential implications for peacekeeping outcomes. The impact of peacekeeping on war-torn nation-states is likely to differ, depending on the forms of peacekeeping. In other words, traditional peacekeeping is unlikely to have the same impacts than multidimensional peacekeeping.

5. UN peacekeeping is a dynamic process that involves not solely the UN, but also other actors facing conflicting issues within particular contexts of time and space. Peacekeeping usually occurs in situations of war-torn societies where conflicting parties with power disparity struggle over difficult relationships. Therefore, analysts could anticipate that the outcome of peacekeeping might be a function of a number of variables related to the characteristics of peacekeeping operations and to those of conflicts.

# Chapter 2

# Data Sources, Database, and Study Variables

This chapter presents the analytical framework and the research methodology that guide this study. This study has adopted a quantitative approach to studying factors that may contribute to peacekeeping success, because (1) principles of quantitative methodology are more likely to help policymaking improve the practice of peacekeeping on a large scale, (2) the use of quantitative techniques sets a steady empirical foundation for significant predictions about the determinants of success in UN peacekeeping, (3) quantitative methods allow the evaluation and comparison of a large number of peacekeeping missions (Diehl 1993; see Druckman and Stern 1997). Doing so ultimately helps transcend the limited use of empirical analytical methods to study UN peacekeeping.

## The Dataset

This research is aimed at transcending the conceptual and methodological limitations previously discussed, specifically the narrow scope of most analyses on peacekeeping, the limited use of empirical analytical methods to study peacekeeping, and the contradictions in assessing peacekeeping outcome.

Any study on international peacekeeping must admit the high costs associated with erroneous conclusions based on subjective judgments. Hence, the analyst ought to set a steady empirical foundation for significant predictions about the determinants of success in UN peacekeeping. To some extent, the use of quantitative techniques helps the analyst meet this requirement because these techniques allow the evaluation and comparison of a large number of peacekeeping missions.

This study seeks to build a dataset with explicit information that could help predict the determinants of UN peacekeeping success. The dataset includes specific information on the context of UN-authorized peacekeeping operations and the process of those operations. The information in the dataset reflects variables characterizing armed conflicts and variables characterizing UN peacekeeping operations, which affect peacekeeping outcome. Quantitative assessments are performed on the dataset to identify which factors contribute to peacekeeping success. This research uses descriptive statistics, frequencies and cross tabulations to present the characteristics of UN peacekeeping. We mainly resort to factor analysis as the most suitable technique of assessment to depict parsimoniously the characteristics of UN peacekeeping. *Factor analysis* provides statistical computations aimed at reducing the characteristics of a sample into small categories or factors that summarize and reflect the initial characteristics (Harman 1967). As a technique largely used in mathematics and psychology to unveil patterns among the variations in values of several variables, *factor analysis* represents a distinctive approach to multivariate analysis. It generates independent factors that correlate highly with several variables (Harman 1967; Babbie 2004; Ho 2006). The purpose of *factor analysis* is to look for commonalities among variables so that a large number of variables could be narrowed down to fewer variables or factors that solve the same problem.

This research examines variations among three clusters of variables with explicit operational criteria: the characteristics of armed conflicts, the characteristics of UN peacekeeping operations, and the outcome variable of peacekeeping.

The characteristics of armed conflicts refer to a series of factors, including *conflict type*, *conflict intensity*, *conflict duration*, and *conflict issues*. It is expected that the intensity of conflict, its duration, and the issues involved in conflict (*secession* or *non-secession*) will affect peacekeeping outcome to some extent.

The characteristics of the peacekeeping operation refer to a series of variables that depict the peacekeeping operation from its beginning (the design of its mandate) to its end (the withdrawal). They include the *mandate*, the *duration*, the *waiting and preparation time*, the *total spending in US$*, the *number of military and police personnel deployed*, the *number of civilian deployed*, the *number of countries contributing troops*, the *percentage of great powers involvement*, the *era of the operation*, and the *region of deployment*. Here, it is expected that the time of intervention of the peacekeeping mission might have some impact on the operation outcome. The moment when the peacekeeping operation has been deployed (early in the conflict versus late in the conflict) may influence peacekeeping outcome. Likewise, the duration of the operation may affect peacekeeping outcome. It is also expected that the mandate of the mission (ceasefire monitoring and observation/military activities versus multidimensional activities/military and civilian activities) might influence peacekeeping outcome. Finally, it is expected that the size of the operation and the resources used (number of uniformed personnel deployed, number of civilian staff deployed, number of troop-contributing countries, total spending) might affect peacekeeping outcome.

Coding the variables in terms of the characteristics of peacekeeping and the characteristics of conflicts allows the analyst to explore the relationships among them and to examine their effect on UN peacekeeping outcome. The outcome variable is the dependent variable (*success* or *failure*). The study examines which process and context variables contribute to the success or failure of UN peacekeeping.

Considering peacekeeping as a form of conflict management and a strategy for conflict resolution, this study links the literature on conflict management (especially the literature on mediation and negotiation) to that of peacekeeping.

In this regard, this research tends to build upon scholars of conflict management who previously studied factors that affect effective mediation (*e.g.* Bercovitch 1991; Bercovitch et al. 1991; Bercovitch and Houston 1993, 1996), and successful negotiation (*e.g.* Druckman et al. 1999; Jackson 2000).

Given differences among studies on peacekeeping in terms of the spatio-temporal domains covered, the coding systems used, this research has developed an original dataset of UN peacekeeping covering a temporal domain from 1956 to 2006, and a relatively broad spatial domain that encompasses 46 peacekeeping operations, including 17 operations in Africa, 8 operations in the Americas, 8 operations in Asia and Pacific, 7 operations in Europe, and 6 operations in the Middle East. Those 46 peacekeeping operations fall under the category of *past operations* as opposed to *current operations* on the website of the UN Department of Peacekeeping Operations. The study has chosen to focus only on *past operations* because they have clear beginning and end dates which facilitate the data collection and foster substantive consistency. *Past operations* have wrapped up, and they allow an easy access to data from the UN website and other relevant sources, more so than *current operations*, which represent ongoing UN peacekeeping operations. It is difficult to get clear data on *current operations* because they are ongoing with dynamic data, subject to change. The decision was made, after a survey we have conducted on the website of the UN Department of Peacekeeping Operations revealed that *current operations* fail to provide much of the data needed for a meaningful study, primarily because they are still running. For instance, it is difficult to have clear figures about the *total spending* of ongoing operations. As a result, the study has excluded all *current operations*.

In the process of compiling its original dataset, the study uses data on peacekeeping and conflict from the website of the United Nations Department of Peacekeeping Operations (DPKO), from Durch's (1993) book on *The Evolution of UN Peacekeeping: Case Studies and Comparative Analysis*, and from Doyle and Sambanis's (2006) book on *Making War and Building Peace: United Nations Peace Operations*. Primary events data sources include UN Secretary General's reports on peacekeeping activities and qualitative evaluations, Resolutions of the Security Council, documents from the *Peacekeeping Best Practices Unit* of the UN, and a series of books and journal articles, including the following: Bellamy, Williams, and Griffin's 2005; Stedman, Rothchild, and Cousens 2002; Druckman and Stern 1997; Diehl, Druckman, and Wall 1998; Bercovitch et al 1991; Jackson 2000; Greig and Diehl's 2005. Data on conflict were taken from Bercovitch and Fretter's (2004) *Regional Guide to International Conflict and Management from 1945 to 2003*, and from Balencie, J. M. & Grange, A. (de La). (1999). *Mondes Rebelles: Guerres Civiles et Violences politiques*. Data on conflict were also taken from the UCDP/PRIO Armed Conflict Dataset (Gleditsch et al. 2002). More specific data collection information is provided for each variable in sections that follow.

# The Unit of Analysis and Coding System

The unit of analysis used in this study is the individual *UNPKO*. As previously indicated, the study examines the characteristics of 46 UNPKOs, covering cases of interstate conflicts as well as intrastate conflicts, which are presented below, in chronological order:

The *United Nations Emergency Force I (UNEF I)* took place in the Middle East from November 1956 to June 1967 (Cold War era). It deployed 6,073 military personnel from 10 countries, with no troop contribution from the five permanent members of the UN Security Council (France, United Kingdom, United States, Russia, and China, hereinafter referred to as "the UNSC 5"). Initiated two weeks after the beginning of the conflict and tasked with monitoring ceasefire and observation, the operation lasted 127 months and cost US$214.2 million (DPKO website 2008).

The *United Nations Observation Group in Lebanon (UNOGIL)* took place from June 1958 to December 1958 (Cold War era). Initiated one month after the start of the conflict, it deployed 591 military personnel from 20 countries, with no troop contribution from the UNSC 5. Two senior civilian staff supported the military personnel. The operation lasted 6 months and cost US$3.7 million. Its mandate revolved around ceasefire monitoring and observation (DPKO website 2008).

The *United Nations Operation in the Congo (ONUC)* took place from July 1960 to June 1964 (Cold War era). Established 9 days after the beginning of the conflict, the operation deployed 19,828 military personnel from 30 countries, with no troop contribution from the UNSC 5. The operation also deployed 4 senior civilian staff. Mandated to perform multidimensional activities, it lasted 48 months and cost US$400.1 million (DPKO website 2008).

The *United Nations Security Force (UNSF)* in West New Guinea took place from October 1962 to April 1963 (Cold War era). Established 9 months after the start of the conflict, the operation deployed 1500 military personnel from 3 countries, with the United States contributing 33.33% of the troops. The operation lasted 7 months and cost US$26.4 million. Its mandate was multidimensional (DPKO website 2008).

The *United Nations Yemen Observation Mission (UNYOM)* took place from July 1963 to September 1964 (Cold War era). Established 7 days following the beginning of the conflict, it deployed 189 military personnel and 48 civilian staff from 11 member states, with no troop contribution from the UNSC 5. Tasked with ceasefire monitoring and observation, it lasted 15 months and cost US$1.8 million (DPKO website 2008).

The *Mission of the Representative of the Secretary General in the Dominican Republic (DOMREP)* took place from May 1965 to October 1966 (Cold War era). Established 21 days after the start of the conflict, it deployed 3 military personnel from 3 countries and one civilian staff, with no troop contribution from the UNSC 5. The operation lasted approximately 18 months and cost US$275,831 (DPKO website 2008).

The *United Nations India-Pakistan Observation Mission (UNIPOM)* took place from September 1965 to March 1966 (Cold War era). Established 48 days following the start of the conflict, it deployed 96 military personnel from 22 countries, with no troop contribution from the UNSC 5, lasted 7 months and cost US$1.7 million. Its functions encompassed ceasefire monitoring and observation (DPKO website 2008).

The *United Nations Emergency Force II (UNEF II)* in the Middle East took place from October 1973 to July 1979 (Cold War era). Established 19 days following the beginning of the conflict, it deployed 6,973 military personnel from 13 countries, with no contribution from the UNSC 5. With a mandate of monitoring ceasefire and observation, the operation lasted 70 months and cost US$446.5 million (DPKO website 2008).

The *United Nations Good Offices Mission in Afghanistan and Pakistan (UNGOMAP)* took place from May 1988 to March 1990 (Cold War era). Established 101 months following the start of the conflict, it deployed 50 military personnel from 10 countries and 2 senior civilian staff, with no troop contribution from the UNSC 5. Tasked with monitoring ceasefire and observation, the mission lasted 23 months and cost US$14 million (DPKO website 2008).

The *United Nations Iran-Iraq Military Observer Group (UNIIMOG)* took place from August 1988 to February 1991 (Cold War era). Established 103 months after the start of the conflict, it mobilized 400 military personnel from 26 countries and 198 civilian staff members, with no troop contribution from the UNSC 5. It had a ceasefire monitoring and observation mandate, lasted 31 months and cost US$177.9 million (Durch 1993; DPKO website 2008).

The *United Nations Angola Verification Mission I (UNAVEM I)* took place from January 1989 to June 1991 (Cold War era). Established 160 months following the start of the conflict, it mobilized 70 military personnel from 10 countries and 37 civilian staff members, with no troop contribution from the UNSC 5. It had a monitoring ceasefire and observation mandate, lasted 30 months and cost US$16,404,200 (Durch 1993; DPKO website 2008).

The *United Nations Transition Assistance Group (UNTAG)* in Namibia took place from April 1989 to March 1990 (Cold War era). Deployed 282 months after the start of the conflict, it mobilized 5,993 military and police personnel from 50 countries, and 3,000 civilian staff members. France, the Soviet Union and United Kingdom contributed 8% of the troops. With a multidimensional mandate, the operation lasted 11 months and cost US$368.6 million (DPKO website 2008).

The *United Nations Observer Group in Central America (ONUCA)* took place from November 1989 to January 1992 (post-Cold War era). Established 87 months after the start of the conflict, it deployed 1098 military personnel from 11 countries and 183 civilian staff members, with no troop contribution from the

UNSC 5. It had a multidimensional mandate, lasted 27 months and cost US$92.4 million (Durch 1993; DPKO website 2008).

The *United Nations Iraq-Kuwait Observation Mission (UNIKOM)* took place from April 1991 to October 2003 (post-Cold War era). Established 7 months following the start of the conflict, it deployed 1,187 military personnel from 36 countries and 177 civilian staff members. China, France, the Russian Federation, United Kingdom, and the United States contributed 13.88% of the troops. With a monitoring ceasefire and observation, the mission lasted 150 months and cost US$600 million (DPKO website 2008).

The *United Nations Angola Verification Mission II (UNAVEM II)* took place from June 1991 to February 1995 (post-Cold War era). Established 189 months after the start of the conflict, it deployed 490 military and police personnel from 25 countries and 365 civilian staff members, with no troop contribution from the UNSC 5. With a multidimensional mandate, it lasted 45 months and cost 175,802,600 (DPKO website 2008).

The *United Nations Observer Mission in El Salvador (ONUSAL)* took place from July 1991 to April 1995 (post-Cold War era). Established 176 months following the start of the conflict, it deployed 683 military and police personnel from 17 countries and 1,220 civilian staff members. (The percentage of great powers involvement was 5.88, with France contributing troops). With a multidimensional mandate, it lasted 46 months and cost US$107.7 million (DPKO website 2008).

The *United Nations Advance Mission in Cambodia (UNAMIC)* took place from October 1991 to March 1992 (post-Cold War era). Established 155 months after the start of the conflict, it deployed 1,090 military personnel from 24 countries and 34 civilian staff members. With China, France, United Kingdom, the Russian Federation, and the United States contributing troops, the percentage of great powers involvement reached 20.83. With a multidimensional mandate, it lasted 6 months (DPKO website 2008).[i]

The *United Nations Protection Force (UNPROFOR)* in the former Yugoslavia took place from February 1992 to March 1995 (post-Cold War era). Established 7 months after the start of the conflict, it deployed 39,402 military and police personnel from 37 countries and 4,632 civilian staff members. With France, United Kingdom, the Russian Federation and the United States contributing troops, great powers involvement was 10.81%. With a multidimensional mandate, the operation lasted 47 months and cost US$4,616,725,556 (DPKO website 2008).

The *United Nations Transitional Authority in Cambodia (UNTAC)* took place from March 1992 to September 1993 (post-Cold War era). Established 159 months following the start of the conflict, it deployed 19,350 military and police personnel from 45 countries and 50,900 civilian staff members. The percentage of great powers involvement was 11.11, with China, France, United Kingdom, the Russian Federation, and the United States contributing troops. With a multidimensional mandate, it lasted 19 months and cost US$1.6 billion (DPKO website 2008).

The *United Nations Operation in Somalia I (UNOSOM I)* took place from April 1992 to March 1993 (post-Cold War era). Established 48 months following the start of the conflict, it deployed 947 military personnel from 16 countries and at least 3 civilian staff members, with no troop contribution from the UNSC 5. With a multidimensional mandate, it lasted 12 months and cost US$ 42.9 million (DPKO website 2008).

The *United Nations Operation in Mozambique (ONUMOZ)* took place from December 1992 to December 1994 (post-Cold War era). Established 207 months after the beginning of the conflict, it deployed 7,663 military and police personnel from 40 countries, and approximately 1,761 civilian staff members. With China, the Russian Federation and the United States contributing troops, the percentage of great powers involvement was 7.5%. With a multidimensional mandate, it lasted 24 months and cost US$ 486.7 million (DPKO website 2008).

The *United Nations Operation in Somalia II (UNOSOM II)* took place from March 1993 to March 1995 (post-Cold War era). Established 60 months after the start of the conflict, it deployed 28,000 military and police personnel from 34 countries and 2,800 civilian staff members. With France and the United States contributing troops, great powers involvement was 5.88%. With a multidimensional mandate, it lasted 24 months and cost US$1.6 billion (DPKO website 2008).

The *United Nations Observer Mission in Uganda-Rwanda (UNOMUR)* took place from June 1993 to September 1994 (post-Cold War era). Established 33 months after the beginning of the conflict, it deployed 81 military personnel from 9 countries, with no troop contribution from the UNSC 5. With a monitoring ceasefire and observation, it lasted 16 months and cost US$2.3 million (DPKO website 2008).

The *United Nations Observer Mission in Liberia (UNOMIL)* took place from September 1993 to September 1997 (post-Cold War era). Established 46 months after the start of the conflict, it deployed 368 military personnel from 22 countries and 284 civilian staff members. With China and the Russian Federation contributing troops, great powers involvement was 9.09%. With a multidimensional mandate, it lasted 48 months and cost US$ 99.3 million (DPKO website 2008).

The *United Nations Mission in Haiti (UNMIH)* took place from September 1993 to June 1996 (post-Cold War era). Established 24 months following the start of the conflict, it deployed 6,912 military and police personnel from 34 countries and 460 civilian staff members. With France, the Russian Federation and the United States contributing troops, great powers involvement was 8.82%. With a multidimensional mandate, it lasted 34 months and cost US$320 million (DPKO website 2008).

The *United Nations Assistance Mission for Rwanda (UNAMIR)* took place from October 1993 to March 1996 (post-Cold War era). Established 36 months following the start of the conflict with a multidimensional mandate, it deployed 2,548 military and police personnel from 40 countries and 376 civilian staff members. The involvement of major powers was 5% with the Russian Federation and United Kingdom contributing troops. It lasted 30 months and cost US$453.9 million (DPKO website 2008).

The *United Nations Aouzou Strip Observer Group (UNASOG)* between Chad and Libya took place from May 1994 to June 1994 (post-Cold War era). Established 256 months after the start of the conflict, with a monitoring ceasefire and observation mandate, it deployed 9 military personnel from 6 countries and 6 civilian staff members, with no troop contribution from the UNSC 5. It lasted one month and cost US$64,471 (DPKO website 2008).

The *United Nations Mission of Observers in* Tajikistan *(UNMOT)* took place from December 1994 to May 2000 (post-Cold War era). Established 32 months after the start of the conflict with a monitoring ceasefire and observation mandate, it deployed 81 military and police personnel from 15 countries and 7 senior civilian staff members, with no troop contribution from the UNSC 5. It lasted 66 months and cost US$63.9 million (DPKO website 2008).

The *United Nations Angola Verification Mission III (UNAVEM III)* took place from February 1995 to June 1997 (post-Cold War era). Established 234 months after the start of the conflict, it deployed 4,220 military and police personnel from 30 countries and at least 2 civilian staff members. With France and the Russian Federation contributing troops, the involvement of major powers was 6.6%. With a multidimensional mandate, it lasted 29 months and cost US$887,196,700 (DPKO website 2008).

The *United Nations Confidence Restoration Operation in Croatia (UNCRO)* took place from May 1995 to January 1996 (post-Cold War era). Established 46 months after the beginning of the conflict, it deployed 7,071 military and police personnel. We did not get reliable data on the countries that contributed troops. Data on the total spending are also missing. Tasked with a multidimensional mandate, the operation lasted 9 months (DPKO website 2008).

The *United Nations Preventive Deployment Force (UNPREDEP)* in the Former Yugoslav Republic of Macedonia took place from March 1995 to February 1999 (post-Cold War era). Established 44 months after the start of the conflict, it deployed 1,110 military and police personnel from 27 countries and 203 civilian staff members. The involvement of great powers was 7.40% with the Russian Federation and the United States contributing troops. With a monitoring ceasefire and observation mandate, it lasted 48 months and cost US$100.5 million (DPKO website 2008).

The *United Nations Mission in Bosnia and Herzegovina (UNMIBH)* took place from December 1995 to December 2002 (post-Cold War era). Established 53 months after the start of the conflict, it deployed 2,047 military and police personnel from 47 countries and 1,569 civilian staff members. With the five permanent members of the Security Council contributing troops, the involvement of major powers was 10.6%. With a multidimensional mandate, it lasted 84 months. Data on its cost were missing (DPKO website 2008).

The *United Nations Transitional Administration for Eastern Slavonia, Baranja and Western Sirmium (UNTAES)* in Croatia took place from January 1996 to January 1998 (post-Cold War era). Established 54 months after the start of the conflict, it deployed 5,561 military and police personnel from 36 countries and 1,003 civilian staff members. With France, United Kingdom, the Russian Federation, and the United States contributing troops, the involvement of major powers was 11.11%. It had a multidimensional mandate, lasted 24 months and cost US$435.2 million (DPKO website 2008).

The *United Nations Mission of Observers in Prevlaka (UNMOP)* took place from January 1996 to December 2002 (post-Cold War era). Established 55 months following the start of the conflict, it deployed 28 military personnel from 22 countries. The involvement of great powers was 4.54% with the contribution of the Russian Federation in troops. With a multidimensional mandate, it lasted 84 months. We did not get reliable data on its cost (DPKO website 2008).

The *United Nations Support Mission in Haiti (UNSMIH)* took place from July 1996 to July 1997 (post-Cold War era). Established 57 months after the start of the conflict, it deployed 1,588 military and police personnel from 13 countries and 289 civilian staff members. France, the Russian Federation and the United States contributed troops, which made the involvement of major powers reach 23.07%. With a multidimensional mandate, it lasted 12 months and cost US$ 62.1 million (DPKO website 2008).

The *United Nations Verification Mission in Guatemala (MINUGUA)* took place from January 1997 to May 1997 (post-Cold War era). Established 506 months after the start of the conflict, it deployed 132 military personnel from 16 countries and 13 civilian staff members. The involvement of major powers was 12.5% with the Russian Federation and the United States contributing troops. It had a multidimensional mandate, lasted 5 months and cost US$ 3.9 million (DPKO website 2008).

The *United Nations Observer Mission in Angola (MONUA)* took place from June 1997 to February 1999 (post-Cold War era). Established 261 days after the start of the conflict, it deployed 3,568 military and police personnel from 36 countries and at least 2 civilian staff members. With France and the Russian Federation contributing troops, the involvement of great powers was 5.5%. With a multidimensional mandate, it lasted 21 months and cost US$ 300.3 million (DPKO website 2008).

The *United Nations Transition Mission in Haiti (UNTMIH)* took place from August 1997 to November 1997 (post-Cold War era). Established 71 months after the start of the conflict, it deployed 300 military and police personnel from 12 countries and at least 1 civilian staff member. The involvement of great powers was 16.66% with France and the United States contributing troops. With a multidimensional mandate, it lasted 4 months and cost US$ 20.6 million (Check DPKO website 2008).

The *United Nations Civilian Police Mission in Haiti (MIPONUH)* took place from December 1997 to March 2000 (post-Cold War era). Established 75 months after the start of the conflict, it deployed 300 police personnel from 11 countries and 222 civilian staff members. The involvement of major powers was 18.18% because France and the United States contributed troops. With a multidimensional mandate, it lasted 28 months and cost US$ 20.4 million (DPKO website 2008).

The *United Nations Civilian Police Support Group (UNPSG)* in Croatia took place from January 1998 to October 1998 (post-Cold War era). Established 79 months after the start of the conflict, it deployed 114 police personnel from 18 countries and 218 civilian staff members. With the Russian Federation and the United States contributing police personnel, the involvement of major powers was 11.11%. With a monitoring ceasefire and observation mandate, it lasted 10 months and cost US$ 28.65 million (DPKO website 2008).

The *United Nations Mission in the Central African Republic (MINURCA)* took place from April 1998 to February 2000 (post-Cold War era). Established 24 months after the start of the conflict, it deployed 1,374 military and police personnel from 14 countries and 238 civilian staff members. The involvement of major powers was 7.14% with France contributing troops. With a multidimensional mandate, it lasted 23 months and cost US$ 101.3 million (DPKO website 2008).

The *United Nations Observer Mission in Sierra Leone (UNOMSIL)* took place from July 1998 to October 1999 (post-Cold War era). Established 89 months after the start of the conflict, it deployed 209 military and police personnel from 28 countries and 55 civilian staff members. China, France, United Kingdom, and the Russian Federation contributing troops, the involvement of major powers reached 14.28%. It had a multidimensional mandate, lasted 16 months and cost US$ 53.1 million (DPKO website 2008).

The *United Nations Mission in Sierra Leone (UNAMSIL)* took place from October 1999 to December 2005 (post-Cold War era). Established 105 months after the start of the conflict, it deployed 17,455 military and police personnel from 39 countries and 874 civilian staff members. The involvement of great powers was 10.25% with China, United Kingdom, the Russian Federation and the United States contributing troops. It had a multidimensional mandate, lasted 75 months and cost US$ 2.8 billion (DPKO website 2008).

The *United Nations Transitional Administration in East Timor (UNTAET)* took place from October 1999 to May 2002 (post-Cold War era). Established 292 months after the start of the conflict, it deployed 7,687 military and police personnel from 49 countries and 2,482 civilian staff members. With China, United Kingdom, the Russian Federation and the United States contributing troops, the involvement of major powers represented 8.16%. With a multidimensional mandate, it lasted 32 months and cost US$ 476.8 million (DPKO website 2008).

The *United Nations Mission of Support in East Timor (UNMISET)* took place from May 2002 to May 2005 (post-Cold War era). Established 324 months after the start of the conflict, it deployed 6,250 military and police officers from 54 countries and 1,773 civilian staff members. The involvement of major powers represented 7.40% because United Kingdom, the Russian Federation and the United States contributed troops. With a multidimensional mandate, it lasted 36 months and cost US$ 565,497,900 (DPKO website 2008).

The *United Nations Operation in Burundi (ONUB)* took place from June 2004 to December 2006 (post-Cold War era). Established 191 months after the start of the conflict, it deployed 5,665 military and police personnel from 50 countries. The involvement of great powers was 4% as China and Russia contributed troops. With a multidimensional mandate, it lasted 31 months and cost US$ 678.3 million (DPKO website 2008).

These 46 UNPKOs were used to intervene in 29 different armed conflicts.[ii] The countries that hosted more than one peacekeeping operations are: the former Yugoslavia 6 (*UNCRO, UNPROFOR, UNPREDEP, UNMIBH, UNMOP, and UNPSG*); Angola 4 (*UNAVEM I, UNAVEM II, UNAVEM III, and MONUA*); Haiti 4 (*UNMIH, UNSMIH, UNTMIH, and MIPONUH*); Somalia 2 (*UNOSOM I and UNOSOM II*); Sierra Leone 2 (*UNOMSIL and UNAMSIL*); Cambodia 2 (*UNAMIC and UNTAC*); and East Timor 2 (*UNTAET and UNMISET*).

The following table shows the coding system with all data items.

*Table 2.1: Coding System*

| Variable Labels | Value *Labels* |
|---|---|
| PKOMAN = Peacekeeping Operation Mandate | *1*'Ceasefire Monitoring/Observation' *2*'Multidimensional activities' |
| PKODUR = Duration of Peacekeeping Operation | *1*'Less than or equal to 12 months'; *2*'>12 months to 24 months'; *3*'>24to36months'; *4*'>36 to 48 months'; *5*'>48 months' |
| NUMIPO = Total Number of Military and Police Personnel Deployed | *1*'Less than or equal to 1000'; *2*'>1000 to 5000'; *3*'>5000 to 10000'; *4*'>10000 to 15000'; *5*'>15000 |
| NUCIST = Number of Civilian Staff | *1*'Less than or equal to 200'; *2*'>200 to 1200'; *3*'>1200 to 2200'; *4*'>2200 to 3200'; *5*'>3200 |
| NUCOCO = Total Number of Countries Contributing Military and Police | *1*'Less than or equal to 10'; *2*'>10 to 20'; *3*'>20 to 30'; *4*'>30 to 40'; *5*'>40' |
| TOSPEND = Total Spending in US Dollars | *1*'Less than or equal to US$100 million'; *2*'>100 to 200 million'; *3*'>200 to 300 million'; *4*'>300 to 400 million'; *5*'>400 |
| CONTYPE = Type of Conflict | *1* 'Intrastate Conflict'; *2* 'Interstate |
| TONUFA = Total Number of Fatalities in Conflict | *1*'Less than or equal to 100000'; *2*'>100000 to 200000'; *3*'>200000 to 300000'; *4*'>300000 to 400000'; *5*'>400000 |
| PKOTIME = Time between the Start of Conflict and the Start of PKO (Days from start of conflict) | *1*'Less than or equal to 1000 days'; *2*'>1000 to 2000'; *3*'>2000 to 3000'; *4*'>3000 to 4000'; *5*'>4000' |
| CONIS = Conflict Issue | *1* 'Non Secession'; *2* 'Secession' |
| PEGREP = Percentage of Great Powers Involved | *1*'Less than or equal to 1%'; *2*'>1 to 5%'; *3*'>5 to 10'; *4*'>10 to 15%'; *5*'>15% |
| CONDUR = Conflict Duration (Number of Days) | *1*'Less than or equal to 1000 days'; *2*'>1000 to 2000'; *3*'>2000 to 3000'; *4*'>3000 to 4000'; *5*'>4000' |
| PKORE = Region of Peacekeeping Operation | *17* 'Africa'; *8* 'America, Asia and Pacific'; *7* 'Europe'; *6* 'Middle East' |
| PKERA = Era of Peacekeeping Operation | *1* 'Cold War Era'; *2* 'Post-Cold War Era' |
| PKOUT = Peacekeeping Outcome | *1* 'Failure'; *2* 'Success' |

# The Dependent Variable: Nature of Peacekeeping Operation Outcome

The UN has initiated 59 peacekeeping missions in the time period covered by our study (from 1956 through 2006). The 46 UNPKOs included in our study were created to help resolve interstate as well as intrastate conflicts. Some of these operations took place in the bipolar international system that resulted in the Cold War, and others took place in the post-Cold War era. Some of them had a mandate that is characterized as involving traditional peacekeeping practices while others are represented as multidimensional peacekeeping. The UN itself considers some of these operations as *successful* while it regards the others as *unsuccessful*.

Struggling to find a common ground about criteria for evaluating success or failure in peacekeeping, academics and practitioners stand by relatively developed indicators. In that logic, Brown (1993) sets two criteria for assessing peacekeeping success: (1) whether the peacekeeping operation facilitates the resolution of underlying disputes, and (2) whether it reduces conflict. In the same vein, Diehl (1993) suggests two criteria to measure success in peacekeeping: the first criterion is the ability of the peacekeeping operation to stop violent hostilities; the second criterion is its ability to advance conflict resolution (Diehl 1993; Johansen 1994; Druckman and Stern 1997; Stedman and Downs 2002). Johansen (1994) rejects the criteria suggested by Diehl (1993) for evaluating peacekeeping and argues that such criteria unfairly exaggerate the burdens on peacekeepers' shoulders because peacekeeping is not aimed at preventing war and resolving conflict (Johansen 1994; Druckman and Stern 1997). Johansen calls upon scholars to measure peacekeeping not against an ideal state of peace or conflict resolution, but rather against the effect of peacekeeping on local populations and situations (Johansen 1994, Druckman and Stern 1997). These competing arguments demonstrate that it can be challenging to develop a catalogue of successful peacekeeping outcomes.

In order to avoid the common trappings of evaluators' bias that, in our opinion, is at the root of the sharp divergences of views about the assessment of peacekeeping operations in the literature on peacekeeping, we decided to use the UN's own determination of whether a UNPKO is successful or not. We are aware that the success or lack of success of a peacekeeping operation may be perceived differently by the policymakers at the UN and other related agencies representing the *international community*, the parties involved in a conflict, the peacekeepers themselves, or outside observers.[iii]

Following the standards of the United Nations, this research considers to be successful any peacekeeping mission that has fulfilled its initial mandate as stated by the United Nations. A mission that fails to do so is considered unsuccessful. To identify which mission was successful and which was not, the research surveys the respective mandates and accomplishments of all 46 peacekeeping operations. For this purpose, we used data from the website of the UN Department of Peacekeeping Operations, assessed the missions' mandates and achievements, using the annual reports of the Secretary-General on peacekeeping. The study also relies on data from Durch (1993), MacQueen (2002), Bellamy, Williams and Griffin (2004) and Doyle and Sambanis (2006) for the same purpose. Depending on the mandate, indicators of success include the signing of formal peace agreements between the disputing parties, the cessation or absence of fighting, and the respect of ceasefire by the parties.

According to UNDPKO, 25 of the 46 operations selected for this study are *successful,* and the other 21 operations are *unsuccessful.*

The successful operations are:

The *United Nations Emergency Force I (UNEF I)*: Deployed in November 1956, *UNEF I* was mandated "to secure and supervise the cessation of hostilities, including a withdrawal of the armed forces of France, Israel and the United Kingdom from Egyptian territory and, after the withdrawal, to serve as a buffer between the Egyptian and Israeli forces, and provide impartial supervision of the ceasefire" (DPKO website 2008; UN General Assembly Resolution 1000, 5 November 1956). The mission was a success. By December 1956, the withdrawal of French and British contingents was completed. Three months later, Israeli forces followed suit and left the Suez Canal area. Following the withdrawal, *UNEF I* effectively controlled the vacated Suez Canal zone, supervised the Canal clearing operations, and set up observations posts along the ceasefire lines to patrol the border areas and to deter possible incursions (Bellamy et al. 2004, p. 106; DPKO website 2008).

The *United Nations Security Force (UNSF)*: *UNSF* was established in October 1962 to maintain peace and security in New West Guinea (West Irian), under the *United Nations Temporary Executive Authority (UNTEA)* established by agreement between Indonesia and the Netherlands on August 15, 1962. The agreement provided that the Secretary-General would supply a *United Nations Security Force (UNSF)* to assist *UNTEA* with as many troops as possible. *UNSF* would monitor the implementation of the ceasefire to ensure an easy implementation of *UNTEA*'s mandate. In the event, *UNSF* effectively monitored the ceasefire and helped ensure law and order during the transition period (DPKO website 2008).

The *Mission of the Representative of the Secretary General in the Dominican Republic (DOMREP)*: Established in May 1965, *DOMREP* was tasked to observe the situation and to report on breaches of the ceasefire between the two *de facto* authorities that controlled the Dominican Republic. Together with his Military Adviser and a small team of military observers, the Representative of the Secretary-General observed and reported on developments in the Dominican Republic, including the signing of an Act of Reconciliation by the contending factions, the establishment of a provisional government and preparations for the general elections. On 1 June 1966, a new President was elected and, in October 1966, *DOMREP* withdrew at the request of the new Dominican government, which expressed satisfaction at the achievements of the UN mission (DPKO website 2008).

The *United Nations India-Pakistan Observation Mission* (*UNIPOM*): *UNIPOM* was established in September 1965 to supervise the ceasefire along the India-Pakistan border (except in the State of Jammu and Kashmir) and the withdrawal of all armed personnel to the positions they had held prior to 5 August 1965. From January through February 1966, *UNIPOM* carefully oversaw the withdrawal activities of Indian and Pakistani troops, which were completed on February 25, 1966. With the withdrawal provisions of the Security Council's resolutions fulfilled by both parties, *UNIPOM* was terminated on March 22, 1966 (DPKO website 2008).

The *United Nations Emergency Force II* (*UNEF II*): Established in October 1973, *UNEF II* was mandated to supervise the ceasefire between Egyptian and Israeli forces and, following the conclusion of the agreements of 18 January 1974 and 4 September 1975, to supervise the redeployment of Egyptian and Israeli forces and to monitor the buffer zones established under those agreements. The deployment of *UNEF II* effectively brought the crisis to an end. Between December 1973 and February 1976, *UNEF II* oversaw activities of disengagement of Egyptian and Israeli forces, the withdrawal of Israeli forces from occupied territory in the Sinai, and the set-up of a buffer zone controlled by the peacekeeping forces. *UNEF*'s mandate was renewed and extended from time to time by the Security Council until July 1979 (DPKO website 2008).

The *United Nations Good Offices Mission in Afghanistan and Pakistan* (*UNGOMAP*): Established in May 1988, *UNGOMAP* was to assist in ensuring the implementation of the Agreements on the Settlement of the Situation Relating to Afghanistan and, in this context, to investigate and report on possible violations of any of the provisions of the Agreements. The mandate of *UNGOMAP* was: i) to monitor non-interference and non-intervention by the parties in each other's affairs; ii) to supervise the withdrawal of Soviet troops from Afghanistan; and iii) to assist the voluntary return of refugees. *UNGOMAP* oversaw the two-phased withdrawal of Soviet forces between May 1988 and February 1989, monitored issues of non-interference and non-intervention from both sides, and cooperated with the *United Nations High Commissioner for Refugees* (*UNHCR*) for the return of a limited number of refugees to Afghanistan. Having completed its job, *UNGOMAP* ceased operations on March 15, 1990 (DPKO website 2008).

The *United Nations Angola Verification Mission I* (*UNAVEM I*): Established in December 1988, *UNAVEM I* was tasked to verify the withdrawal of Cuban forces from the territory of Angola, in accordance with the timetable agreed upon by the governments of Cuban and Angola. *UNAVEM I* effectively monitored the phased withdrawal of 50,000 Cuban troops from Angola. The withdrawal was completed by 25 May 1991, more than a month ahead of schedule (DPKO website 2008).

The *United Nations Transition Assistance Group* (*UNTAG*): Established in April 1989, *UNTAG* was mandated to assist the Special Representative of the Secretary-General to: i) ensure the independence of Namibia through free and fair elections under the supervision and control of the United Nations; ii) monitor the withdrawal and demobilization of all military forces in Namibia, the release of political prisoners, and the reform of law and order; and finally iii) to facilitate the return of Namibian refugees. Between April 1989 and March 1990, *UNTAG* ensured a smooth and successful electoral process and monitored the ceasefire between the *South West Africa People's Organization* (*SWAPO*) and South African forces, as well as the withdrawal and demobilization of all military forces in Namibia. Political prisoners were released and discriminatory laws were abolished. In the process, the *United Nations High Commissioner for Refugees* helped repatriate 34,000 Namibians. Independent Namibia joined the United Nations in April 1990 (Bellamy et al. 2004; DPKO website 2008).

The *United Nations Observer Mission in El Salvador* (*ONUSAL*): Established in July 1991, *ONUSAL* was mandated to verify the implementation of all agreements between the Government of El Salvador and the *Frente Farabundo Martí para la Liberación Nacional* (*FMLN*). The agreements involved a ceasefire, the reform and reduction of the armed forces, the creation of a new police force, the reform of the judicial and electoral systems, human rights, land tenure and other economic and social issues. Between July 1991 and April 1995, *ONUSAL* worked actively to complete its mandate. *ONUSAL* monitored the accords and verified the demobilization of combatants, their reintegration into society and the respect by both parties of their human rights commitments. *ONUSAL* also worked for a reduction by 50% of the Salvadoran army and the departure of officers allegedly responsible for human rights violations. Moreover, *ONUSAL* assisted in reforming the judicial system, the national police, training the new civilian police, and implementing land reform policies. *ONUSAL* successfully supervised the 1994 general elections (Bellamy et al. 2004; DPKO website 2008).

The *United Nations Advance Mission in Cambodia* (*UNAMIC*): *UNAMIC* was created in October 1991 with the mandate to assist the Cambodian parties in maintaining their ceasefire in preparation for the establishment of the *United Nations Transitional Authority in Cambodia* (*UNTAC*), and to initiate mine-awareness training of civilian populations. In January 1992, the mandate was enlarged to include a major training program for Cambodians in mine-detection and mine-clearance and the mine-clearing of repatriation routes, reception centers and resettlement areas. Between November 1991 and March 1992, in spite of the multiple challenges it encountered, *UNAMIC* completed the different elements of its mandate to prepare the ground for *UNTAC*. The functions of *UNAMIC* were subsumed by *UNTAC* in March 1992 (DPKO website 2008).

The *United Nations Transitional Authority in Cambodia (UNTAC)*: Deployed in March 1992, *UNTAC* was tasked to ensure the implementation of the Agreements on the Comprehensive Political Settlement of the Cambodia Conflict, signed in Paris on October 23, 1991. Its mandate included the promotion of human rights, the organization and conduct of general elections, military arrangements, civil administration, the maintenance of law and order, the repatriation and resettlement of refugees and displaced persons, and also the rehabilitation of Cambodian infrastructure. From March 1992 through September 1993, *UNTAC* completed its mandate through its control of Cambodia's administrative structures, including foreign affairs, defense, security, finance and communications in order to build a stable environment. The supervision of free and fair national elections in May 1993 served as a clear indicator of success for the mission. In the process, *UNHCR* oversaw the repatriation and resettlement of some 360,000 refugees and displaced persons. *UNTAC*'s mandate ended in September 1993 with the promulgation of a Constitution and the formation of a new Government for Cambodia (Bellamy et al. 2004; DPKO website 2008).

The *United Nations Operation in Mozambique (ONUMOZ)*: *ONUMOZ* was created in December 1992 to help implement the General Peace Agreement signed by the President of the Republic of Mozambique and the President of the *Resistência Nacional Moçambicana*. Its mandate was to: i) monitor the ceasefire, the separation, concentration and demobilization of combatants, and the collection, storage and destruction of weapons; ii) verify the complete withdrawal of foreign forces and provide security in the transport corridors; iii) monitor and verify the disbanding of private and irregular armed groups; iv) authorize security arrangements for vital infrastructures and provide security for United Nations and other international activities in support of the peace process; v) provide technical assistance and monitoring for the entire electoral process; vi) coordinate humanitarian assistance to refugees, internally displaced persons, demobilized military personnel and otherwise affected local populations. From December 1992 to December 1994, *ONUMOZ* worked actively to accomplish its mandate. In addition to monitoring the implementation of the military dimensions of the Peace Agreement and supervising the electoral process, the operation initiated a humanitarian assistance program for the resettlement of the 3.7 million Mozambicans displaced by war. In 1993, the *UNHCR* launched the repatriation of 1.3 million refugees. About 75% of the internally displaced persons had been resettled and most refugees had returned to Mozambique by mid-1994. More than 76,000 soldiers from both parties were demobilized, 10,000 of which *ONUMOZ* helped integrate into the new national army. The mission also recovered about 155,000 weapons and monitored Mozambique's first multiparty elections in October 1994. The new Parliament was inaugurated on December 8, 1994, and the new President sworn in one day later, on December 9 (DPKO website 2008).

The *United Nations Aouzou Strip Observer Group* (*UNASOG*): UNASOG was created in May 1994 with the mandate to monitor the withdrawal of the Libyan administration and forces from the Aouzou Strip in accordance with the decision of the *International Court of Justice*. From May 4 through May 30, 1994, the mission successfully accomplished its mandate with the collaboration of the governments of Chad and Libya (DPKO website 2008).

The *United Nations Mission of Observers in Tajikistan* (*UNMOT*): Established in December 1994, *UNMOT*'s initial mandate was to monitor the ceasefire agreement between the Government of Tajikistan and the United Tajik Opposition. In 1997, after the parties signed the general peace agreement, the mandate was expanded to include supervision of its implementation. From December 1994 to May 2000, the mission accomplished the different tasks that were assigned to it and completed its mandate successfully (DPKO website 2008).

The *United Nations Confidence Restoration Operation in Croatia (UNCRO)*: UNCRO was established in March 1995 with the mandate to: i) oversee the implementation of the ceasefire agreement of March29, 1994 in Croatia; ii) help to implement the economic agreement of December 2, 1994; iii) supervise the crossing of military personnel, equipment, supplies and weapons over specified international borders; iv) facilitate the delivery of humanitarian aid to Bosnia and Herzegovina through the territory of Croatia; vi) monitor the demilitarization of the Prevlaka peninsula. The mission successfully achieved all the elements of its mandate from March 31, 1995 through January 15, 1996 (DPKO website 2008).

The *United Nations Preventive Deployment Force (UNPREDEP)*: UNPREDEP was established in March 1995 with the mandate to monitor and report any developments in the border areas which could undermine confidence and stability in the Former Yugoslav Republic of Macedonia and threaten its territory. From March 31, 1995 through February 25, 1999, *UNPREDEP* successfully achieved different elements of its mandate. In addition to monitoring and reporting on the situation along the borders with the Federal Republic of Yugoslavia and Albania, the mission collaborated with civilian agencies to provide community services and humanitarian assistance to the local populations. By the end of 1995, *UNPREDEP* operated dozens of permanent observation posts along a 420-kilometre stretch on the Macedonian side of the border with the Federal Republic of Yugoslavia and Albania. It also operated 33 temporary observation posts, and also about 40 border and community patrols daily. The mission has supported the international community in its efforts to promote a peaceful resolution of the situation in the former Yugoslavia; it has contributed to consolidating mutual dialogue among political parties and assisted in monitoring human rights, as well as inter-ethnic relations; it has conducted successful mediations and overseen negotiations over difficult border issues between the parties; it has established mutually beneficial contacts with the military authorities of Albania and the Federal Republic of Yugoslavia, and at the highest political level of Albania. Overall, the mission has played important preventive roles (DPKO website 2008).

The *United Nations Transitional Administration for Eastern Slavonia, Baranja and Western Sirmium (UNTAES)*: Established on January 15, 1996, *UNTAES* was mandated to administer Eastern Slavonia, Baranja and Western Sirmium by working to ensure their integration into Croatia. The tasks of the mission included supervising and facilitating demilitarization; monitoring the return of refugees; contributing to the maintenance of peace and security; setting up a temporary police force; assuming civil administration and public services; organizing general elections; promoting human rights; monitoring the demining of the area; and coordinating activities of economic reconstruction and development of the region. After repeated extensions of its mandate, *UNTAES* successfully achieved its objectives on January 15, 1998 (DPKO website 2008).

The *United Nations Mission of Observers in Prevlaka (UNMOP)*: UNMOP was established on February 1, 1996 to monitor the demilitarization of the Prevlaka peninsula, a strategic area disputed by Croatia and the Federal Republic of Yugoslavia. From February 1, 1996 through December 15, 2002, the mission successfully fulfilled its mandate: it oversaw the demilitarization of the Prevlaka peninsula and of the neighboring areas in Croatia and the Federal Republic of Yugoslavia; it maintained dialogue with the local authorities in order to strengthen liaison, and reduce tensions; it worked to improve security and to promote confidence building (DPKO website 2008).

The *United Nations Verification Mission in Guatemala (MINUGUA)*: Created on January 20, 1997, *MINUGUA* was mandated to verify the Olso Agreement on the Definitive Ceasefire between the Government of Guatemala and the *Unidad Revolucionaria Nacional Guatemalteca (URNG)*. Its functions revolved around the observation of a formal cessation of hostilities, the separation and concentration of the respective forces, and the disarmament and demobilization of *URNG* combatants. From March 3, 1997 through May 14, 1997, the mission successfully completed its mandate. It supervised the separation of forces between the Guatemalan Army and *URNG*, and collected weapons, munitions, explosives, mines and related military equipment from former combatants. 2,928 *URNG* combatants were demobilized and 535,102 weapons and ammunition rounds were collected by *MINUGUA*. On May 14, 1997, *URNG* weapons, munitions and equipment, as well as the lists of destroyed explosive devices, were handed over to the Ministry of the Interior. The former combatants were all issued temporary identification cards. The mission also monitored the clearing of minefields. By April 18, 1997, 378 mines and explosive devices had been lifted and destroyed (DPKO website 2008).

The *United Nations Civilian Police Support Group (UNPSG)*: UNPSG was established in January 1998 with the mandate to continue monitoring the performance of the Croatian police in the Danube region, particularly with respect to the return of displaced persons. From January 16 through October 15, 1998, the mission successfully achieved its mandate by undertaking policing tasks in the region. *UNPSG* effectively contributed to preventing the return of instability to the region (DPKO website 2008).

The *United Nations Mission in the Central African Republic (MINURCA)*: *MINURCA* was deployed in April 1998 to assist in maintaining and enhancing security and stability in Bangui and surrounding areas; supervise, control storage, and monitor the disposition of weapons retrieved in disarmament exercise; assist national security forces in capacity-building and maintaining law and order in Bangui; provide advice and technical support for legislative elections. The mission was later mandated to provide support to the presidential elections and to oversee the destruction of confiscated weapons. From April 15, 1998 through February 15, 2000, *MINURCA* successfully achieved its goals. The mission helped restore a climate of stability and security for dialogue among political actors. This outcome incited the international financial institutions to stimulate the Central African Republic's economy; it also enabled the holding of peaceful legislative elections in November and December 1998. *MINURCA* also provided support to the presidential elections of September 1999. The mission carried out other peace-building activities in accordance with its mandate for stability and socio-economic reforms in the country (DPKO website 2008).

The *United Nations Mission in Sierra Leone (UNAMSIL)*: UNAMSIL was created on 22 October 1999 to help the government of Sierra Leone and the rebels implement the *Lomé Peace Agreement* and to monitor the implementation of the disarmament, demobilization and reintegration activities. Specifically, the mission was tasked to: i) set a presence at key locations throughout the territory of Sierra Leone, including at disarmament/reception centres and demobilization centres; ii) ensure the security and freedom of movement of UN personnel; iii) monitor the ceasefire; iv) promote confidence-building; v) support the provision of humanitarian assistance; vi) back the Special Representative of the Secretary-General and his staff, human rights officers and civil affairs officers; vii) and supervise the national elections in Sierra Leone. The mission's mandate was revised consecutively on February 7, 2000, on May 19, 2000 and on March 30, 2001, to providing security at government buildings, major intersections, airports and other key locations; facilitating the free movement of people, goods and humanitarian assistance; monitoring disarmament, demobilization and reintegration activities, and assisting in maintaining law and order. From October 1999 through December 2005, *UNAMSIL* successfully completed its mandate. By early 2002, it had disarmed and demobilized more than 75,000 ex-fighters, including child soldiers. It provided logistics and public information support to help organize Sierra Leone's first ever free and fair presidential and parliamentary elections, and facilitated the voluntary return of more than half a million refugees and internally displaced persons. It contributed to the restoration of public administration, social services and law and order. It monitored training in human rights and helped set up the Special Court for Sierra Leone to try war criminals. It assisted the Government in establishing a

*Truth and Reconciliation Commission.* In collaboration with UN agencies, UNAMSIL also initiated projects to provide jobs to thousands of unemployed youth and former combatants and basic services to local communities (Bellamy et al. 2004; DPKO website 2008).

The *United Nations Transitional Administration in East Timor (UNTAET)*: UNTAET was established on 25 October 1999 to administer the territory of East Timor, exercise legislative and executive authority during the transition period, and support capacity-building for self-government. The specific tasks of the mission included: i) providing security and maintaining law and order in East Timor; ii) establishing an effective administration; iii) assisting in the development of civil and social services; iv) coordinating humanitarian assistance, rehabilitation and development assistance; v) promoting capacity-building for self-government; vi) assisting in the establishment of conditions for sustainable development. The mission successfully completed its mandate on May 20, 2002, the day East Timor became an independent country (DPKO website 2008).

The *United Nations Mission of Support in East Timor (UNMISET)*: UNMISET was established on May 20, 2002 to assist newly independent East Timor (Timor-Leste) in attaining self-sufficiency. The mission was mandated to: i) assist major administrative structures that are significant to the viability and stability of East Timor; ii) provide temporary law enforcement and public security, and contribute to the development of a new law enforcement agency in East Timor (the East Timor Police Service); and iii) assist in maintaining the external and internal security of East Timor. From May 20, 2002 through May 20, 2005, *UNMISET* successfully achieved the different requirements of its mandate (DPKO website 2008).

The *United Nations Operation in Burundi (ONUB)*: ONUB was established on May 21, 2004 to support and help Burundi implement efforts for sustainable peace and national reconciliation. The mission's specific tasks included: i) monitoring ceasefires; ii) developing confidence-building; iii) coordinating disarmament, demobilization and reintegration activities; iv) creating conditions for the safe delivery of humanitarian assistance and facilitating the voluntary return of refugees and internally displaced persons; v) ensuring a secure environment for free, transparent and peaceful elections in Burundi; vi) protecting civilians from violence and promoting human rights; vii) ensuring the security of UN personnel, facilities, installations and equipment, as well as the security and freedom of movement of *ONUB*'s personnel; viii) helping reform the judiciary and correction system; and ix) extending State authority and utilities throughout the territory, including police and judicial institutions. *ONUB* successfully completed its mandate on 31 December 2006 (DPKO website 2008).

The following operations are considered unsuccessful:
1. The *United Nations Observation Group in Lebanon (UNOGIL)*;

2. The *United Nations Operation in the Congo (ONUC)* (Bellamy et al. 2004; DPKO website 2008);
3. The *United Nations Yemen Observation Mission (UNYOM)*;
4. The *United Nations Iran-Iraq Military Observer Group (UNIIMOG)*;
5. The *United Nations Observer Group in Central America (ONUCA)*;
6. The *United Nations Iraq-Kuwait Observation Mission (UNIKOM)* (Bellamy et al. 2004; DPKO website 2008);
7. The *United Nations Angola Verification Mission II (UNAVEM II)*;
8. The *United Nations Protection Force (UNPROFOR)* (Bellamy et al. 2004; DPKO website 2008);
9. The *United Nations Operation in Somalia I (UNOSOM I)* (Bellamy et al. 2004; DPKO website 2008);
10. The *United Nations Operation in Somalia II (UNOSOM II)* (Bellamy et al. 2004; DPKO website 2008);
11. The *United Nations Observer Mission in Uganda-Rwanda (UNOMUR)*
12. The *United Nations Observer Mission in Liberia (UNOMIL)*;
13. The *United Nations Mission in Haiti (UNMIH)*;
14. The *United Nations Assistance Mission for Rwanda (UNAMIR)* (Bellamy et al. 2004; DPKO website 2008);
15. The *United Nations Angola Verification Mission III (UNAVEM III)*;
16. The *United Nations Mission in Bosnia and Herzegovina (UNMIBH)*;
17. The *United Nations Support Mission in Haiti (UNSMIH)*;
18. The *United Nations Observer Mission in Angola (MONUA)*;
19. The *United Nations Transition Mission in Haiti (UNTMIH)*;
20. The *United Nations Civilian Police Mission in Haiti (MIPONUH)*;
21. The *United Nations Observer Mission in Sierra Leone (UNOMSIL)* (Bellamy et al. 2004; DPKO website 2008).

The dependent variable, *peacekeeping operation outcome*, is labeled 'PKOUT'. Successful operations are coded '2' and unsuccessful ones are coded '1'.

# The Independent Variables

The 14 independent variables selected for this study reflect characteristics of the armed conflicts that made the UNPKO necessary on one hand, and characteristics of the UNPKO itself on the other hand. The independent variables reflecting conflict characteristics include the *nature or type of conflict*, the *duration of the conflict*, the *number of fatalities from that conflict* (or *conflict intensity*), and the major *issues of the conflict*. The independent variables that depict the characteristics of UN peacekeeping operations are: the *nature of the mandate of the peacekeeping operation*, the *time of peacekeeping intervention*, the *duration of peacekeeping operation*, the *total number of military and police personnel deployed*, the *total number of civilian staff deployed*, the *total number of countries contributing troops*, the *percentage of involvement of permanent members of the Security Council*, and the *total spending in US dollars*.

In other words, the variables used in this study mirror the underlying dimensions of the hypothesis of our research. The 14 variables encompass nominal, ordinal, and ratio levels variables. However, for the purpose of homogeneity, which represents a conceptual assumption underlying factor analysis (Ho 2006), all ratio level variables are transformed into ordinal level variables with five categories (coded 1-2-3-4-5) in this study. All nominal variables in the study are two-category nominal variables (coded 1-2), except the *region of peacekeeping operation* which has four categories.

The following paragraphs inform the reader more about each of the 14 independent variables and their measurements.

## Conflict Characteristics

This study examines a total of 29 armed conflicts situations, comprising 10 interstate conflicts and 19 intrastate conflicts that required the deployment of 46 of the 59 peacekeeping operations conducted by the UN between 1956 and 2006. The decision to select each of the 46 UNPKOs included in our study was informed by the on-going debate occurring in the international relations literature about what constitutes an armed conflict situation that is pertinent for scholarly study.

According to the authors of the *Correlates of War (COW) project*, which has served for decades as the main data source for longitudinal studies on armed conflict, an armed conflict is an interstate or intrastate conflict with a minimum of 1,000 battle related deaths (Singer and Small 1972, 1982, and 1994). Noting that the 1,000 battle related deaths criterion set a very high threshold, which led to the exclusion of some important intrastate conflicts from such studies, Regan defined an *intrastate* conflict as a conflict which involves battles between two mobilized groups and in which the total number of fatalities reaches a minimum of 200 deaths (Regan 2002).

In an attempt to address the limitations of the COW project data, the *Department of Peace and Conflict Research* at Uppsala University and the *International Peace Research Institute of Olso (PRIO)* co-sponsored the creation of an armed conflict dataset that included armed conflicts with a significantly lower number of battle-related deaths. The *Uppsala Conflict Data Project (UCDP)/PRIO dataset* defines an armed conflict as "contested incompatibility that concerns government or territory or both where the use of armed force between two parties results in at least 25 battle-related deaths", with at least one of the parties being the government of a state (Gleditsch et al. 2002, pp. 618-619).

Despite its substantial efforts in defining armed conflict with a lower, threshold of 25 battles related casualties, the UCDP/PRIO dataset is also exclusive of armed conflict with casualties levels lower than 25 battle-related deaths. Moreover, one can argue that the distinction observed between government and territory in the definition is not relevant because the two categories are not mutually exclusive, but overlapping. A government is usually attached to a territory and vice-versa. Therefore, a conflict involving one issue also involves the other. This study defines armed conflict as fighting between two or more mobilized groups (of which at least one is the government of a state) in which arms are used and where there are battle-related deaths. Such fighting revolves or not around issues of secession or autonomy. This definition of armed conflict is more inclusive than the definition by the UCDP/PRIO dataset. In addition, our definition of armed conflicts indicates that conflict issues revolve around secession and non-secession.

Rather than simply using traditional databases such as the *Correlates of War (COW) Project* (Singer and Small 1994) or the UCDP/PRIO Armed Conflicts Dataset (Gleditsch et al. 2002), which represent standard data sources for systematic work on conflict, this study designs an original dataset that meets the criteria of our definition of armed conflict, which is more inclusive and allows us to examine UN peacekeeping operations in countries that would have been excluded otherwise, Haiti for instance. The COW datasets use a relatively high threshold of 1,000 battle-related deaths to define war, which excludes well-known conflicts with lower death tolls. The UCDP/PRIO Armed Conflict Dataset lowers the threshold to 25 battle-related fatalities.

This study adopts a threshold lower to 25 battle-related deaths. The UCDP/PRIO Armed Conflict Dataset does not include Haiti in the cases covered, whereas this study examines Haiti in order to evaluate UN peacekeeping efforts in that country. In addition, the COW dataset covers the period from 1816 to 1992, while the dataset in this study covers the period from 1956 to 2006. As the UCDP/PRIO Armed Conflict Dataset has suggested in its critics of the COW project, extending the analysis to a very long period may raise problems of theoretical inconsistency, including the fact that the meaning of certain variables in the 1820 might be different from what it means in the 1980s (Gleditsch et al. 2002, p. 617). The coding systems used in the *Correlates of War Project* and the *UCDP/PRIO Armed Conflict Dataset* are different from the coding system used in this study.

The sources that the study uses for data collection allow the compilation of an original dataset that focuses essentially on 29 situations of conflicts that are of interest for this work, including 10 interstate and 19 intrastate conflicts that have recorded 46 UN peacekeeping interventions from 1956 to 2006. This dataset allows an examination of the characteristics of UN peacekeeping operations, using a comparative approach to exploring conflicts that have witnessed the deployment of UN peacekeeping operations in the time period covered.

There is a broad consensus in the conflict analysis and resolution literature that the outcome of any conflict management initiative will be determined by the characteristics of the conflict that justifies and requires the initiative (Ott 1972; Kressel and Pruitt 1989; Bercovitch et al. 1991; Jackson 2000). Since peacekeeping operations are essentially conflict management initiatives, and we are interested in identifying the major determinants of UNPKO success, we decided that our factor analytic model should include the following four variables, which represent the most important characteristics of the conflicts that prompted the deployment of the selected UNPKOs as we have indicated previously: i) the nature or type of the conflict (whether it qualifies as an interstate or an intrastate conflict); ii) the duration of the conflict; iii) the number of fatalities that resulted directly from that conflict; and iv) the nature of the major conflict issues.

### Nature or Type of Conflict: Interstate or Intrastate Conflict

An interstate conflict is a militarized dispute between two or more states, whereas an intrastate conflict involves fighting between two organized groups within the same state (Diehl and Goertz 2000; Regan 2002; Small and Singer 1982; Gleditsch et al. 2002). Greig and Diehl have concluded that the presence of peacekeeping forces differently affects the probability of occurrence and the likelihood of success of mediation and negotiation initiatives in interstate conflicts than in intrastate conflicts (Greig and Diehl 2005). This finding supports our expectation that the success of a UNPKO itself could depend on whether the operation is deployed in an interstate or intrastate conflict situation.

Data on this variable were taken from Bercovitch and Fretter 2004; from the UN Department of Peacekeeping Operations (DPKO) website; from Balencie & de La Grange 1999; and from the *UCDP/PRIO Armed Conflict Dataset*, Version 4-2007 (Gleditsch et al. 2002).

The 10 interstate conflicts included in this study are:

1. *The Suez Canal war between Egypt on one hand and the United Kingdom, France and Israel on the other, from October to November 1956.* This war over the ownership of the Suez Canal lasted 7 days (less than 1 month) and caused more than 6,000 battle related deaths (Bercovitch and Fretter 2004; DPKO website 2008).

2. *The conflict between Indonesia and the Netherlands over the administration of West New Guinea, from January to August 1962.* This conflict erupted from a separatist mobilization of Indonesia against the Netherlands in an effort to remove West New Guinea from the control of the Netherlands. It lasted for about 8 months and caused 30,000 deaths (Bercovitch and Fretter 2004; DPKO website 2008).

3. *The second Kashmir war between India and Pakistan from August to September 1965.* This conflict erupted between India and Pakistan over territorial rivalries surrounding Kashmir's secessionist ambitions. It lasted 48 days (less than two months) and caused more than 7,000 deaths (Bercovitch and Fretter 2004; DPKO website 2008).

4. *The Yom Kippur War opposing Israel to Egypt and Syria in October 1973.* This conflict erupted when Egypt and Syria launched the 1973 offensives in an attempt to win back the Sinai and the Golan Heights, which Israel had taken from them by force in 1967. It lasted 16 days

(less than a month) and caused 11,200 deaths (Bercovitch and Fretter 2004; DPKO website 2008).

5.  *The Iran-Iraq war over the Shatt al-Arab Waterway from February 1980 to March 1989*. This conflict erupted when Iraq invaded the disputed Shatt al-Arab region with the intention of forcing Iran to cede that region. It lasted for about 119 months and caused more than 1 million deaths (Bercovitch and Fretter 2004; DPKO website 2008).

6.  *The Namibian war of independence against South Africa from 1976 through 1989*. This conflict erupted when the South West African People's Organization (SWAPO) started hostilities in an attempt to remove Namibia from South Africa's control. It lasted approximately 291 months and caused about 13,000 deaths (Durch 1993; Bercovitch and Fretter 2004; DPKO website 2008).

7.  *The regional wars in Central America from September 1982 through August 1987*. These conflicts erupted as a result of a series of guerilla insurgencies and civil wars in Costa Rica, El Salvador, Guatemala, Honduras and Nicaragua, that created instability in the region in the 1980s. They lasted approximately 60 months and caused about 225,000 deaths (Bercovitch and Fretter 2004; DPKO website 2008).

8.  *The Gulf War from August 1990 to May 1991*. This conflict erupted as a result of Iraq's invasion of Kuwait to materialize its long held claim of the territory of Kuwait as its 19th province. It lasted 9 months and caused about 100,000 deaths (Bercovitch and Fretter 2004; DPKO website 2008).

9.  *The conflict between Chad and Libya over the Aouzou Strip*. This conflict erupted when Libya annexed the Aouzou strip in northern Chad in an attempt to forcefully settle existing borders disputes. It lasted about 255 months and caused 250 deaths (Bercovitch and Fretter 2004; DPKO website 2008).

10. *East Timor's independence war against Indonesia from October 1975 to May 2002*. This conflict erupted when East Timorese separationists started hostilities in an attempt to gain independence from Indonesia, which wanted to integrate the island by force into its territory. It lasted 324 months and caused 200,000 deaths. (Bercovitch and Fretter 2004; DPKO website 2008).

The 19 intrastate conflicts included in this study are:

1.  *The civil war in Lebanon from May 1958 to June 1959*. This conflict erupted as a result of an armed struggle for political power between several rival factions, but did not evolve into a secession war. It lasted 13 months and caused more than 1,300 deaths (Bercovitch and Fretter 2004; DPKO website 2008).

2.  *The civil war in Congo (the former Zaire and current Democratic Republic of Congo) from July 1960 to June 1964*. This conflict resulted in the secession of the mineral-rich province of Katanga. It lasted 48

months and caused more than 110,000 deaths (Bercovitch and Fretter 2004; DPKO website 2008).

3. *The civil war in Yemen from September 1962 to October 1967.* This conflict started as a rebellion, but did not evolve into a secession war. It lasted 62 months and caused more than 100,000 deaths (Bercovitch and Fretter 2004; DPKO website 2008).

4. *The civil war in the Dominican Republic from April 1965 to September 1966.* This conflict started as a rebellion, but did not evolve into a secession war. It lasted 21 days (less than a month) and caused 3,500 deaths (Bercovitch and Fretter 2004; DPKO website 2008).

5. *The civil war in Afghanistan from December 1979 to September 2001.* This conflict erupted as a civil war, but then led to the invasion of Afghanistan by the Soviet Union. It lasted 252 months and caused about 1.5 million deaths (Bercovitch and Fretter 2004; DPKO website 2008).

6. *The secession war in Angola from 1975 to 2002.* This conflict erupted when the *Front for the Liberation of the Enclave of Cabinda (FLEC)* started hostilities against Portuguese colonial authorities and the *Popular Movement for the Liberation of Angola (MPLA)* in an attempt to gain independence for the enclave of Cabinda during Angola's civil war. It lasted about 327 months and caused up to 1.5 million deaths (Bercovitch and Fretter 2004; Balencie and Grange 1999; DPKO website 2008).

7. *The civil war in El Salvador from 1977 to 1992.* This conflict did not involve any secessionist claims. It lasted about 193 months and caused more than 75,000 deaths (Balencie and Grange 1999; Bercovitch and Fretter 2004; DPKO website 2008).

8. *The civil war in Cambodia from January 1979 to May 1991.* This conflict erupted as a civil war with no secessionist claims, but then led to the invasion of Cambodia by Vietnam. It lasted approximately 155 months and caused about 500,000 deaths (Balencie and Grange 1999; Bercovitch and Fretter 2004; DPKO website 2008).

9. *The secession wars in the former Yugoslavia from 1989 through 1995.* This conflict erupted as a result of sharp ethnic rivalries that manifested after the fall of the Berlin Wall and the subsequent collapse of (the Soviet Union and) the former Yugoslavia. The members of the Federation of Yugoslavia (Bosnia-Herzegovina, Croatia, Macedonia, Montenegro, Serbia, and Slovenia) seceded and declared independence one after another. These ethnic wars lasted 54 months and caused at least 250,000 deaths (Bercovitch ad Fretter 2004; Balencie and Grange 1999; DPKO website 2008).

10. *The civil war in Somalia from 1988 to 2004.* This conflict erupted as a civil war with widespread episodes of clan-based violence, and then led to the secession of Somaliland from Somalia. It lasted 194 months and

caused more than 200,000 deaths (Balencie and Grange 1999; Bercovitch and Fretter 2004; DPKO website 2008).

11. *The civil war in Mozambique from 1976 to 1992.* This conflict erupted as a result of an armed struggle for power between rival political groups, and did not involve any secessionist claims. It lasted 205 months and caused about 1 million deaths (Balencie and Grange 1999; Bercovitch and Fretter 2004; DPKO website 2008).

12. *The civil war in Rwanda from October 1990 to July 1994.* This conflict erupted as a result of ethnic violence that led to and followed the assassination of the President of the Republic of Rwanda and the collapse of the Rwandese State. It did not involve any secessionist claims, and ultimately led to the genocide of Tutsis by Hutus. It lasted 46 months and caused about 1 million deaths (Balancie and Grange 1999; Bercovitch and Fretter 2004; DPKO website 2008).

13. *The civil war in Liberia from December 1989 to August 1997.* This conflict erupted as a result of a struggle for political power between various armed groups, but then quickly evolved into a civil war that did not involve any secession issues. It lasted 93 months and caused more than 150,000 deaths (Balencie and Grange 1999; Bercovitch and Fretter 2004; DPKO 2008).

14. *The socio-political crisis in Haiti from September 1991 to September 1994.* This conflict erupted as a result of a military coup that resulted in severe socio-political unrest and the breakdown of law and order in Haiti. It lasted 36 months and caused at least 24 deaths. (Balencie and Grange 1999; Bercovitch and Fretter 2004; DPKO website 2008).

15. *The civil war in Tajikistan from April 1992 to June 1997.* This conflict erupted as a result of disintegration of the Soviet Union and the subsequent proclamation of independence in Tajikistan. A civil war involving no secession claims, it lasted 62 months and caused 50,000 deaths (Balencie and Grange 1999; Bercovitch and Fretter 2004; DPKO website 2008).

16. *The civil war in Guatemala from 1961 through 1996.* This conflict was a civil war involving no secession claims. It lasted 505 months and caused more than 100,000 deaths (Balencie and Grange 1999; Bercovitch and Fretter 2004; DPKO website 2008).

17. *The socio-political crisis in the Central African Republic from April 1996 to June 1997.* This conflict erupted as a result of a series of military revolts against the country's government, but never involved any secession claims. It lasted 14 months and caused 254 deaths (Balencie and Grange 1999; DPKO website 2008).

18. *The civil war in Sierra Leone from March 1991 through 1999.* This conflict erupted as a result of contagion from the on-going conflict in the neighboring Liberia. A civil war with no secession claims, it lasted

101 months and caused more than 100,000 deaths (Balencie and Grange 1999; Bercovitch and Fretter 2004; DPKO website 2008).
19. *The ethnic conflict in Burundi from 1988 to 2000.* This conflict was a civil war with no secession claim that evolved to include aspects of genocide. It lasted 146 months and caused 163,300 deaths (Balencie and Grange 1999; Bercovitch and Fretter 2004).

The variable *Type of conflict* is labeled CONTYPE. Each interstate conflict is coded '2' and each intrastate conflict is coded '1'.

## Total Number of Fatalities

The total number of fatalities that are directly related to a conflict situation has been often used as a measure of conflict intensity. There is a strong consensus among conflict analysis and resolution scholars on the fact that the intensity of a conflict is an important factor that may determine the outcome of any conflict management initiative. However, there are persistent disagreements over how conflict intensity influences the outcome of conflict management efforts. Thus, some scholars contend that intensity of a conflict is positively correlated with the likelihood of success of conflict management initiatives (Jackson, 1952 & 2000; Young 1967 & 1968; Bercovitch et. al. 1991) while others find that conflict intensity is negatively correlated with the likelihood of success of conflict management initiatives because higher intensity results in higher entrenchment and polarization of the parties' positions (Modelski, 1964; Burton 1969; Kochan and Jick, 1978; Brockner 1982; Kressel and Pruitt, 1989; Kleiboer, 1996; Jackson, 2000).

For the purposes of this study, we hypothesize that *conflict intensity* determines, to some extent, the success of peacekeeping operations. Conflict intensity is measured here in terms of the *total number of fatalities* registered over the duration of the conflict. Because of the presence of outliers in our dataset (some conflicts have caused less than 25 deaths whereas many conflicts have caused thousands of deaths), this variable, labeled TONUFA, is transformed into (or re-expressed as) an ordinal level variable composed of the following intervals: *1* 'less than or equal to 100000 deaths'; *2* 'more than 100000 to 200000 deaths'; *3* 'more than 200000 to 300000 deaths'; *4* 'more than 300000 to 400000 deaths'; *5* 'more than 400000 deaths'. Data on this variable are taken from Bercovitch and Fretter 2004, and from Balencie & Grange (de La) 1999.

## Conflict Duration

There is a widespread consensus in the conflict analysis and resolution literature that the duration of a conflict affects the chances of success of conflict management initiatives and efforts (Edmead 1971; Northedge and Donelan 1971; Bercovitch et al. 1991). Bercovitch et al. (1991) found that conflict duration is negatively correlated with the likelihood of success of mediation efforts.

For the purposes of this study, we hypothesize that *conflict duration* will influence, to some extent, the likelihood of success of peacekeeping operations. However, we make no claims regarding the direction of the relationship. Conflict duration is measured here in terms of the total number of days between the start of the conflict and the moment when it is considered settled or resolved. Because of the presence of outliers (some conflicts lasted only a few days whereas many conflicts lasted for several years), this variable, labeled CONDUR, is re-expressed as an ordinal level variable composed of the following intervals: *1* 'less than or equal to 1000 days'; *2* 'more than 1000 to 2000'; *3* 'more than 2000 to 3000'; *4* 'more than 3000 to 4000'; *5* 'more than 4000 days'. Data on conflict duration were obtained from Bercovitch and Fretter (2004) and from Balencie & Grange (de La) (1999).

## Conflict Issues

The conflict analysis and resolution literature uses the phrase '*conflict issues*' to designate the underlying causes of a conflict. Conflict issues have often been categorized as related to *ideology, security, sovereignty, self-determination, resources*, and *ethnicity. Ideological conflict* refers to disagreements between parties over fundamental values and beliefs, which are often related to the nature of the political system (capitalism, socialism, democracy, or others) that should be adopted. *Security issues conflict* refers to fighting over territories and borders. *Sovereignty conflict* refers to conflicts in which the parties make incompatible claims to a given territory. *Self-determination conflict* refers to struggles for national liberation and independence. *Resources conflict* refers to conflicts in which the parties compete for the control of the nation's economic and non-economic resources (political power). Finally, *ethnicity conflict* designates conflicts in which the parties display sentiments and interests that are favorable to their own ethnic group and unfavorable to other ethnic groups (Bercovitch et al., 1991; Jackson, 2000; Kellas, 1998).

The analyst can argue that these variables are not mutually exclusive; they are highly correlated. Ethnicity is associated with ideology because it can be perceived as a social construct from a constructivist approach. Sovereignty also relates to ideology when it is perceived as a social construct. Security, ethnicity, resources, sovereignty and self-determination can be associated because an ethnic group in conflict would fight for their needs of security, resources, self-determination, and even sovereignty, which are all interrelated. To some extent, sovereignty, self-determination, ideology, and resources are overlapping.

The *UCDP/PRIO Armed Conflict Dataset* codes *conflict issues* in terms of *government, territory*, or *government and territory* (Gleditsch et al. 2002). These categories are also overlapping because it is difficult and even impossible to separate government and territory. A government is over a territory, and a territory usually has a government, under normal circumstances.

In light of our critical assessment of existing conflict typologies, this study takes a minimal approach to *conflict issues*, and distinguishes only between conflicts involving secessionist claims and conflicts without secessionist claims. Secession has been defined as "any form of withdrawal or separation from membership in or association with a state or an organization" as a sign of de-solidarity vis-à-vis that state or organization and in the quest of self-determination, autonomy, sovereignty or independence (Neufeldt 1997). As this definition clearly indicates, secession conflicts include conflicts involving (often ethnicity-based) claims to national self-determination and, by way of consequence, to state sovereignty.

For the purposes of this study, a secession war is one in which at least one of the parties has expressed the intention of the people it claims to represent to separate and withdraw from one existing state, and to establish a separate state and an independent government over a portion of the territory formerly controlled by the government of that existing state. Obviously therefore, secession conflicts directly involve territorial disputes with ideological, security, resources, and (at least sometimes) ethnicity-centered elements.

We consider a conflict to be a *secession* conflict/war if any such claims were made by one of the parties, regardless of whether that party was successful in achieving its intention to secede. Conflicts where such claims were not made will be assigned to the *non-secession* conflict category.

International conflict management scholars suggest that the nature of conflict issues affects the effectiveness and the likelihood of success of conflict management/resolution initiatives (Lall 1966; Otto 1972; Randle 1973; Bercovitch et al. 1991; Jackson 2000). In their research on the conditions for effective mediation, Bercovitch et al. found that the chances for successful mediation are higher in conflicts involving territorial disputes than in conflicts revolving around ideology and independence (Bercovitch et al. 1991). While we have our doubts about the validity of distinction between territorial disputes and independence and/or ideology-based conflicts, we agree that different conflict issues will affect peacekeeping outcome differently.

The data on the variable *conflict issues* were obtained from Bercovitch and Fretter 2004; Balencie & Grange (de La). 1999; and the UCDP/PRIO Armed Conflict Dataset Version 4-2007 (Gleditsch et al. 2002). The variable is labeled CONIS and coded '2', when the conflict involves secessionist claims, and '1' otherwise.

## Peacekeeping Operation Characteristics

As we have highlighted in previous lines, the characteristics of each UNPKO included in this study are: the nature of the mandate of the peacekeeping operation, the time of peacekeeping intervention, the duration of peacekeeping operation, the total number of military and police personnel deployed, the total number of civilian staff deployed, the total number of countries contributing troops, the percentage of involvement of permanent members of the Security Council, and the total spending in US dollars.

International conflict management scholars agree that the timing of intervention, the type of intervention, and the amount of resources used for intervention affect the outcome of conflict management interventions (Bercovitch, Anagnoson, & Wille 1991, Bercovitch and Jackson 1997, Regan and Stam 2000, Regan 2002).

## Nature of the Peacekeeping Operation's Mandate

Peacekeeping scholars argue that any attempt to assess a peacekeeping operation should focus on the mandate of the operation and its ability to restrain conflict (Diehl 1993; Durch 1993, 1996; Ratner 1995; Druckman and Stern 1997). Diehl, for example, believes that the fulfillment of the operation mandate is a clear standard for evaluating peacekeeping success, and stresses that peacekeeping success should be evaluated against what an operation has achieved and/or how it has been conducted (Diehl 1993).

For the purposes of this study, we hypothesize that the nature of the mandate of a UNPKO will affect the likelihood of success of that operation. The nature of the mandate of a given UNPKO is represented by the following two categories: i) traditional peacekeeping mandate, which is often limited ceasefire monitoring and observation; and ii) multidimensional peacekeeping mandate, which includes more than the activities listed in the first category. The variable of *peacekeeping operation mandate* is labeled PKOMAN. It is coded '1' when the operation has a traditional peacekeeping mandate, and '2' otherwise.

Data on *peacekeeping operation mandate* were obtained from the UN Department of Peacekeeping Operations website; and from internet postings of UN Security Council resolutions and UN Secretary-General's reports on the United Nations' website.

## Time Lag between Start of Conflict and Start of Peacekeeping Intervention

International conflict management scholars agree that the timing of mediation initiatives in the course of a conflict situation influences the chances of success of such initiatives, but disagree on when the right moment for mediation to take place is. Some argue that the probability for mediation success is higher in the early stages of a conflict (Edmead 1971; Kleiboer et al. 1995; Bercovitch and Houston 1996) when others believe that success in mediation is more likely in the later stages (Northedge and Donelan 1971; Ott 1972; Zartman 1985; Jackson 2000).

Bercovitch et al. estimate that the likelihood of mediation success is only 19% in disputes that have lasted for more than 12 months when mediation occurs. They also find, however, that "mediation attempts taking place one to three months into a dispute show a greater chance of success (37%) than those initiated when the conflict is less than one month old (23%)". They conclude, therefore, that success in mediation requires a minimum amount of waiting time before intervention, although longer-lasting conflicts have less chance for successful mediation (Bercovitch, Anagnoson, and Willie, 1991, p. 13).

For the purposes of this study, we hypothesize that the waiting time before the deployment of a UNPKO will affects, to some extent, the probability of success of that operation. *Waiting time before deployment of a peacekeeping intervention* is measured in the number of days from the start date of the conflict to the said deployment. The variable of *timing of peacekeeping operation*, labeled 'PKOTIME', is transformed into an ordinal level variable with the following five intervals: *1* 'less than or equal to 1000 days'; *2* 'more than 1000 to 2000'; *3* 'more than 2000 to 3000'; *4* 'more than 3000 to 4000'; *5* 'more than 4000'. Data on this variable were obtained from the UN Department of Peacekeeping Operations website; Bercovitch and Fretter 2004; and Balencie & Grange (de La) 1999.

## Duration of Peacekeeping Operation

While this has not been clearly established in the international conflict management literature, we hypothesize, for the purposes of this study, that the duration of a peacekeeping operation will affect, to some extent, the chances of success of that operation. *UNPKO duration* is labeled 'PKODUR', and is measured in the number of months. It is then re-expressed as an ordinal level variable with the following five intervals: *1* 'less than or equal to 12 months'; *2* 'more than 12 months to 24 months'; *3* 'more than 24 to 36 months'; *4* 'more than 36 to 48 months'; *5* 'more than 48 months'. Data on this variable were taken from the UNDPO website.

## Total Number of Military and Police Personnel Deployed

It seems logical to expect that the success of a peacekeeping operation will be determined by the number of military and police personnel deployed in that operation. In fact, this appears to be an assumption that is inherent to every decision made in the design and establishment of peacekeeping operations in general, and of traditional peacekeeping operations in particular, in the real world.

For the purposes of this study, we hypothesize that the total number of military and police personnel deployed in a UNPKO will affect, to some extent, the likelihood of success of that operation. The *total number of uniformed personnel* is labeled 'NUMIPO' and is transformed into an ordinal level variable with the following intervals: *1* 'less than or equal to 1000 uniformed personnel'; *2* 'more than 1000 to 5000'; *3* 'more than 5000 to 10000'; *4* 'more than 10000 to 15000'; *5* 'more than 15000'. Data on this variable were obtained from the UNDPO website.

### Total Number of Civilian Staff Deployed

It is also logical to expect that the success of a peacekeeping operation will be determined by the number of civilian staff deployed. In fact, this is the main assumption that justifies the evolution from traditional to multidimensional peacekeeping operations in UNPKO decision-making.

For the purposes of this study, we hypothesize that the total number of civilian staff deployed in a UNPKO will affect, to some extent, the likelihood of success of that operation. The *total number of civilian staff deployed* is labeled 'NUCIST', and is transformed into an ordinal level variable with the following intervals: *1* 'less than or equal to 200'; *2* 'more than 200 to 1200'; *3* 'more than 1200 to 2200'; *4* 'more than 2200 to 3200'; *5* 'more than 3200. Data on this variable were obtained from the UNDPO website, and from Durch 1993.

### Total Number of Countries Contributing Troops

The number of countries contributing troops to a peacekeeping operation is a significant measure of the level of political support within the international community for the peaceful resolution of the conflict that lead to the establishment of the said operation. The idea that a larger number of countries contributing troops will increase the likelihood of success of the operation is also implicit in UNPKO decision-making.

For the purposes of this study, we hypothesize that the total number of countries contributing troops to a UNPKO will affect, to some extent, the likelihood of success of that operation. The *total number of countries contributing troops* is labeled 'NUCOCO'. It is re-expressed as an ordinal level variable with the following intervals: *1* 'less than or equal to 10 countries'; *2* 'more than 10 to 20 countries'; *3* 'more than 20 to 30 countries'; *4* 'more than 30 to 40 countries'; *5* 'more than 40 countries'. Data on the *total number of countries contributing troops* were obtained from the website of the UN Department of Peacekeeping Operations.

### Percentage of Major Powers Involvement

The percentage of permanent members of the UN Security Council (USA, France, United Kingdom, China, and Russia) will determine peacekeeping outcome: the higher the percentage of major powers involved in a peacekeeping operation, the greater the chances of success in that operation. *The percentage of major powers involvement* is divided into five intervals: *1* 'less than or equal to 1%'; *2* 'more than 1 to 5%'; *3* 'more than 5 to 10'; *4* 'more than 10 to 15%'; *5* 'more than 15%. The *percentage of major powers involvement* was calculated by using data on countries contributing troops from the website of the UN Department of Peacekeeping Operations. This variable is labeled 'PEGREP'.

## Total Spending in US Dollars

The total amount of financial resources invested in a peacekeeping operation is positively related to the probability of peacekeeping success. It is logical to suppose that the more money spent for a peacekeeping operation, the greater the chances of success in peacekeeping.

For the purposes of this study, we hypothesize that the total amount of spending in a UNPKO will affect, to some extent, the likelihood of success of that operation. The *total amount of money spent* is labeled 'TOSPEND', and is measured in US dollars. It is transformed into an ordinal level variable with the following intervals: *1* 'less than or equal to US$100 million'; *2* 'more than 100 to 200 million'; *3* 'more than 200 to 300 million'; *4* 'more than 300 to 400 million'; *5* 'more than 400 million US dollars'. Data on this variable were obtained from the UNDPO website.

## Region of Peacekeeping Operation

In the course of our study, we noted that UNPKOs are unequally distributed among the major geopolitical regions composing the globe, with 'Africa' hosting the largest number and percentage of the 46 selected operations (17), followed by 'Asia and Pacific' (8) and 'America' (8), then by Europe (7), and the 'Middle-East' (6) according to the UN's own classification of regions hosting peacekeeping operations (UNDPO website 2008). This observation spurred a desire to determine whether there is a correlation between the geopolitical region in which a peacekeeping operation takes place and the success of that operation.

For the purposes of this study, we hypothesize that the region in which a UNPKO is deployed will affect, to some extent, the likelihood of success of that operation. We choose to treat the variable "region" as a characteristic of the peacekeeping operation itself, rather than of the conflict that made the establishment of the operation necessary, because we are essentially interested in studying variations between UNPKOs and not between the conflicts *per se*. Moreover, we are aware that all conflicts do not lead to the establishment of a UNPKO. Therefore, we are not interested in knowing which regions have armed conflicts that are most amenable to peacekeeping operations, or even which regions have armed conflicts that are most amenable to successful UNPKOs. Instead, we want to know whether some regions are more favorable to the success of a UNPKO than others.

The variable of *region hosting UNPKO* is labeled 'PKORE'. It takes the following values and codes: '17' for Africa; '8' for Asia and Pacific; '8' for America, '7' for Europe; and '6' for the Middle-East. This means that each region is coded with the number of peacekeeping operations it hosted.

Data on the region of peacekeeping operations were obtained from the UNDPO website.

## Era of Peacekeeping Operations

International conflict management and peacekeeping scholars have noted that the post-Cold War era is characterized by a significant surge in the demand for UNPKOs (Greig and Diehl 2005; Regan 2002). Harff and Gurr believe that UN peacekeeping interventions have become more proactive than reactive after the dissolution of the Soviet Union because the remaining great powers are less reluctant to intervene in intrastate conflicts in order to stop human rights violations (Harff and Gurr 2004).

For the purposes of this study, we hypothesize that the time period or era in which a UNPKO is deployed will affect, to some extent, the likelihood of success of that operation. Here again, we choose to treat the variable "era" (time period of occurence) as a characteristic of the peacekeeping operation itself, rather than of the conflict that made it necessary, because we are essentially interested in studying variations between such operations and not between the conflicts *per se*. Knowing that all conflicts do not cause the deployment of UNPKOs, we are not interested in knowing which of the 46 selected armed conflicts are most amenable to peacekeeping operations, or even to successful UNPKOs, but rather whether the cold war era was more favorable to the success of a UNPKO than the post-cold war era, and vice-versa.

The variable of *era of peacekeeping operation*, labeled 'PKOERA', takes the following values: '1' for Cold War era operations; and '2' for post-Cold War era operations. Data on this variable were taken from the UNDPO website.

The next chapter describes the statistical methods used for processing and analysis of the data collected for our study, and presents the results.

## Endnotes

1. We did not get reliable data on the cost of the United Nations Advance Mission in Cambodia (UNAMIC).

2. Some conflict situations were dynamics or required in-depth follow-up by the UN for sustainable peace, which made a few conflict-shattered countries host more than one peacekeeping operations.

3. The study adopts the UN standards because they contribute to preventing conceptual confusions and disagreements that surround the assessment of peacekeeping outcome in the literature. The analyst should be aware that peacekeeping outcome could be perceived differently by the international community, the UN, the parties involved in a conflict, the outside observer, or by the peacekeepers themselves. In addition, peacekeeping outcome could also be perceived as successful in the short term (i.e. during the conduct of the peacekeeping operation or immediately after it ends), and as unsuccessful a few years later (see Greig and Diehl 2005).

# Chapter 3

# Statistical Methods and Results: The Factor Analytic Model

*Factor Analysis* is a series of mathematical techniques used in the empirical sciences to reduce or simply observed data (Harman 1967). In theory and in practice, factor analysis refers to the application of a system of statistical methods to represent a set of variables in terms of a small number of hypothetical variables. As a result, the main objective of factor analysis is "the orderly simplification of a large number of intercorrelated measures to a few representative constructs or factors" (Ho 2006, 203). Harman concurs when he clearly echoes that:

> The principal concern of factor analysis is the resolution of a set of variables linearly in terms of (usually) a small number of categories or "factors". This resolution can be accomplished by the analysis of the correlations among the variables. A satisfactory solution will yield factors which convey all the essential information of the original set of variables. Thus, the chief aim is to attain scientific parsimony or economy of description. (1967, 4)

The basic assumption of *factor analysis* is that there is a small number of underlying dimensions, or factors, that can explain observed covariations or correlations between a larger number of measured variables. In other words, *factor analysis* assumes the existence of the following elements: i) a system of observed (and measured) variables; ii) a system of underlying (i.e., hypothetical or unobservable) source variables, called factors; and iii) a correspondence between these two systems of variables, whereby the measured variables are linear combinations of the underlying source variables (the factors). *Factor analysis* exploits this correspondence to draw conclusions about the unobservable factors (Essis 1997; Kim and Mueller 1978).[i]

*Factor analysis* utilizes a variety of statistical techniques to condense a larger amount of variables into a small amount of hypothetical variables, with the assumption that there are principal factors that can account for covariations between a large amount of variables (Kim and Mueller 1978). The study performed a *principal components analysis* on fourteen variables representing selected characteristics of UN peacekeeping and armed conflicts in order to obtain a small number of factors that stand for the initial fourteen variables.

This study uses *factor analysis* to pursue four major objectives: (1) to assess the correlations among the dependent and independent variables, (2) to address possible issues of multiple collinearity among independent variables, (3) to reduce the large number of 14 independent variables to a small number of explanatory factors, and (4) to test the hypothesis that the characteristics of UN peacekeeping and its outcome can be explained by a small number of factors. Primarily concerned with classification and verification of a clear hypothesis, the ultimate goal of this study is to provide a "parsimonious description of observed data" (Harman 1967, 5) on UN peacekeeping.

A *correlation matrix* was performed on all 15 dependent and independent variables. It shows a significant number of high correlations among the variables. The number of high intercorrelations between the variables indicates the appropriateness of the hypothesized factor model. Other statistical tests were also performed in order to establish the adequacy of our factor analytic model. *Table 3.1* shows the correlation matrix statistics and the associated model adequacy and significance tests results:

*Table 3.1: Correlation Matrix Statistics (Model Adequacy and Significance Tests)*

| | | |
|---|---|---|
| Determinant of Correlation Matrix | = | 0.000 |
| Kaiser-Meyer-Olkin Measure of Sampling Adequacy | = | 0.560 |
| Bartlett's Test of Sphericity Approx. Chi-Square | = | 271.621 |
| Significance Level | = | 0.000 |

*Reproduced Correlation Matrix Summary Results*

### KMO and Bartlett's Test

| Kaiser-Meyer-Olkin Measure of Sampling Adequacy. | | .560 |
|---|---|---|
| Bartlett's Test of Sphericity | Approx. Chi-Square | 271.621 |
| | df | 91 |
| | Sig. | .000 |

This table indicates that the *Correlations Matrix* records a large value for *Bartlett's Test of Sphericity* statistic, at a very low statistical significance level. The meaning of these statistics is that, given the common assumption that the distribution of cases in the true population is multivariate normal, the hypothesis that this *Correlation Matrix* is an identity matrix must be rejected. The *Correlation Matrix* also shows comfortable values for the *Kaiser-Meyer-Olkin (KMO)* measure of sampling adequacy, which compares the magnitude of the observed correlation coefficients with those of the partial correlation coefficients. The relatively large value registered for the overall *KMO* statistic means that the use of a factor analytic model is appropriate for this data.

Another indication of the goodness-of-fit of the factor analytic model is provided by the magnitude of the residuals, that is, the difference between the observed correlation coefficients, for each pair of variables, and the correlation coefficient estimated by the *n-factor model*. This is so because *factor analysis* assumes that the observed correlations between variables are caused by their sharing common factors. It follows that the estimated correlations between the factors and the variables can be used to estimate the correlations between the variables. For each pair of variables, the residual is the difference between the correlation coefficients estimated by a specific factor analytic model and the observed correlation coefficients. The number and magnitude of the residuals indicate how well the fitted model reproduces the observed correlations between variables. If more than half of the residuals in the model are greater than 0.05 in absolute value, then the model does not fit the data well. In our *Armed Conflict and UNPKO Characteristics* factor analytic model, less than half of the residuals are greater than 0.05, in absolute value. Thus, the *4-factor model* must be considered to fit the data very well (Essis 1997, p. 112).

Following the above *correlation matrix* analysis, a *principal components* factor extraction procedure was carried out in order to obtain uncorrelated linear combinations of the observed variables, or *factor loadings*. These *factor loadings* are similar to the standardized regression coefficients in a multiple regression equation, given each of the original variables as the dependent variable, and all the factors as the independent/explanatory variables. If the underlying factors are uncorrelated, the values of the coefficients (loadings) for each variable are not dependent on each other. The loadings are the correlations between the factors and the variables. They represent the unique contribution of each factor to the value of each variable (Essis 1997, p. 113).

*Table 3.2* reproduces the *Final Statistics* section of the *SPSS factor analysis computer output*. The *Communalities* indicate the proportion or amount of variance in each variable that is accounted for by the common factors (Ho 2006). *Initial* communalities are estimates of the variance in each variable accounted for by all components or factors. For principal components extraction, this is always equal to 1.0 for correlation analyses. *Extraction* communalities are estimates of the variance in each variable accounted for by the components.

*Table 3.2: Final Statistics*

Communalities

|  | Initial | Extraction |
|---|---|---|
| Mandate of Peacekeeping Operation | 1.000 | .782 |
| Total Number of Military and Police Deployed | 1.000 | .748 |
| Number of Civilian Staff | 1.000 | .645 |
| Total Number of Countries Contributing Troops | 1.000 | .844 |
| Percentage of Great Powers Involved | 1.000 | .779 |
| Duration of Peacekeeping Operation in Months | 1.000 | .427 |
| Era of Peacekeeping Operation | 1.000 | .578 |
| Type of Conflict | 1.000 | .734 |
| Conflict Issue | 1.000 | .487 |
| Total Spending in US Dollar | 1.000 | .834 |
| Total Number of Fatalities in Conflict | 1.000 | .535 |
| Duration of Conflict in Days | 1.000 | .888 |
| Number of Days between Start of Conflict and Start of PKO | 1.000 | .879 |
| Region of Peacekeeping Operation | 1.000 | .663 |

*Communalities*

|  | Initial | Extraction |
|---|---|---|
| Mandate of Peacekeeping Operation | 1.000 | .782 |
| Total Number of Military and Police Deployed | 1.000 | .748 |
| Number of Civilian Staff | 1.000 | .645 |
| Total Number of Countries Contributing Troops | 1.000 | .844 |
| Percentage of Great Powers Involved | 1.000 | .779 |
| Duration of Peacekeeping Operation in Months | 1.000 | .427 |
| Era of Peacekeeping Operation | 1.000 | .578 |
| Type of Conflict | 1.000 | .734 |
| Conflict Issue | 1.000 | .487 |
| Total Spending in US Dollar | 1.000 | .834 |
| Total Number of Fatalities in Conflict | 1.000 | .535 |
| Duration of Conflict in Days | 1.000 | .888 |
| Number of Days between Start of Conflict and Start of PKO | 1.000 | .879 |
| Region of Peacekeeping Operation | 1.000 | .663 |

Extraction Method: Principal Component Analysis.

The *Total Variance Explained* by the initial solution, extracted components, and rotated components is displayed in *Table 3.3*. In a *Factor Analysis Output*, the *Total Variance Explained* usually provides "the number of common factors computed, the eigenvalues associated with these factors, the percentage of total variance accounted for by each factor, and the cumulative percentage of total variance accounted for by the factors" (Ho 2006, 219).

*Table 3.3 Total Variance Explained*

*Total Variance Explained*

| Compon ent | Initial Eigenvalues | | | Extraction Sums of Squared Loadings | | | Rotation Sums of Squared Loadings[a] |
|---|---|---|---|---|---|---|---|
| | Total | % of Variance | Cumulati ve % | Total | % of Variance | Cumulati ve % | Total |
| 1 | 4.238 | 30.270 | 30.270 | 4.238 | 30.270 | 30.270 | 3.458 |
| 2 | 2.395 | 17.105 | 47.375 | 2.395 | 17.105 | 47.375 | 2.723 |
| 3 | 1.833 | 13.094 | 60.469 | 1.833 | 13.094 | 60.469 | 2.683 |
| 4 | 1.358 | 9.698 | 70.167 | 1.358 | 9.698 | 70.167 | 1.431 |
| 5 | .994 | 7.097 | 77.263 | | | | |
| 6 | .911 | 6.508 | 83.771 | | | | |
| 7 | .664 | 4.745 | 88.516 | | | | |
| 8 | .476 | 3.398 | 91.914 | | | | |
| 9 | .341 | 2.437 | 94.352 | | | | |
| 10 | .257 | 1.836 | 96.188 | | | | |
| 11 | .241 | 1.719 | 97.907 | | | | |
| 12 | .150 | 1.070 | 98.978 | | | | |
| 13 | .099 | .705 | 99.683 | | | | |
| 14 | .044 | .317 | 100.000 | | | | |

Extraction Method: Principal Component Analysis.

a. When components are correlated, sums of squared loadings cannot be added to obtain a total variance.

The first section of *Table 3.3* shows the *Initial Eigenvalues*. The *Total* column presents the *eigenvalue*, or amount of variance in the original variables accounted for by each component. The *% of Variance* column gives the ratio, expressed as a percentage, of the variance accounted for by each component to the total variance in all of the variables. The *Cumulative %* column gives the percentage of variance accounted for by the first *n* components. For example, the cumulative percentage for the second component is the sum of the percentage of variance for the first and second components. For the initial solution, there are as many components as variables, and in a correlations analysis, the sum of the eigenvalues equals the number of components. We requested that *eigenvalues* greater than 1 be extracted, so the first four principal components form the extracted solution.

The second section of the table shows the extracted components. They explain more than 70% of the variability in the original fourteen variables, so one can considerably reduce the complexity of the data set by using these components, with only less than 30% loss of information. The *rotation* maintains the *cumulative percentage* of variation explained by the extracted components, but that variation is now spread more evenly over the components. The large changes in the individual totals suggest that the rotated component matrix will be easier to interpret than the unrotated matrix. The rotated component matrix helps us determine what the components represent.

An *eigenvalue* is the total amount of variance explained by a given factor. It is "a ratio between the common (shared) variance and the specific (unique) variance explained by a specific factor extracted" (Ho 2006, 205). Since there are as many principal components (or factors) as there are variables, and each variable has a variance of 1, a factor with a variance less than 1 has no more data reducing and explanatory power than a single variable (Essis 1997, p. 113). Therefore, only those factors with an *eigenvalue* greater than 1, that is, factors which account for a total amount of variance greater than 1, were retained by the principal components factor extraction procedure. As *Table 3.3* indicates, the first four factors (or *principal components*) explain more than 70 % of the total variance, leaving the remaining 10 factors, together, to account for less than 30 percent of the variance. The results of the *principal components* factor extraction procedure suggest that the *4-factor model* adequately represents the *Armed Conflict and UNPKO Characteristics* data used in this study.

The adequacy of our factor analytic model is further illustrated by the high values of the squared multiple correlation coefficients ($R^2$) between each variable and all the others. Those coefficients indicate the strength of the linear association among the (dependent and) independent variables. The *SPSS Factor Analysis computer output* displays those values as *communalities* for each of the original 14 variables. The *communalities* provide another way to assess the goodness-of-fit of the *n-factor model* by evaluating how well the estimated factors describe the original variables. In effect, the *communality* of a given variable is the proportion of its variance which is explained by the common factors extracted by the *principal components* procedure. A *communality* of 0 indicates that the *n* common factors explain none of the variance of the variable considered, whereas a *communality* of 1 indicates that the common factors explain all the variance. The *communality* value for each variable is the sum of the proportions of its variance which are explained individually by each common factor. The variance that remains unexplained by the *n* factors is called the "uniqueness" of the variable because it is explained by its "unique factor" (Essis 1997, p. 115). In this case, the high communality values displayed in *Table 3.2* indicate that the extracted factors/components do represent the variables well.

Following the *factor extraction* procedure, a *factor rotation* was performed on the 4 factors retained. The *factor rotation* procedure is necessary to simplify the factor structure, and thus to maximize the interpretability of the factors that have been retained. The *rotation procedure* transforms a complex initial factor matrix into a simpler one by increasing the number of large and small factor loadings for the *n* variables included in the model.

The *oblique rotation* method was used, rather than the *orthogonal rotation* method, for the following three reasons. First, the *orthogonal rotation* procedure would 'force' the explanatory factors to be uncorrelated, which the oblique rotation does not. Knowing that the success of a UNPKO (or the lack thereof) is a function of a large number of necessarily interrelated variables or factors, we opted for the *oblique rotation* procedure because it enables our observations to remain as close as possible to the 'natural' state of affairs. Second, the orthogonal and oblique rotation algorithms will both yield the same grouping of variables and, therefore, the interpretation of the factors does not change according to the method used. Third, and most importantly, because it allows for correlation among the factors, *oblique rotation* does, indeed, simplify the resulting factor pattern matrix, therefore yielding substantially meaningful factors (Essis 1997, pp. 115-116).

In order to facilitate the interpretation of the factors, the *rotated factor/component pattern matrix* is sorted in such a way that all the variables with large loadings for a given factor appear together and small factor loadings are omitted. Thus, only loadings greater than 0.5 in absolute value on a given factor are displayed for the relevant variables. In addition, and as a general rule, only variables with high loadings on a single factor have their loadings displayed in the column for the relevant factor.[ii] It is also important to signal that missing values are *excluded cases listwise* in the factor analysis.

*Tables 3.4A, 3.4B, and 3.4C* show the resulting *Factor Component Matrix, Factor Pattern Matrix*, and *Factor Structure Matrix*. The *Component Matrix* reflects the unrotated component analysis matrix. It unveils the correlations relating the variables to the four extracted factors in the forms of coefficients or factor loadings. The *factor loadings* "indicate how closely the variables are related to each factor" (Ho 2006, 219). The *Pattern Matrix* and the *Structure Matrix* both reflect the *oblimin rotated matrix* and show the correlations between variables and factors. However, whereas the correlations presented by the *Structure Matrix* may be contaminated and confusing for interpretation, the *Pattern Matrix* "shows the uncontaminated correlations between variables and factors and is generally used for interpreting factors" (Ho 2006, 220). As a result, this study relied on the Pattern Matrix for interpretation.

*Table 3.4A Component Matrix(a)*

Component Matrix[a]

| | Component | | | |
|---|---|---|---|---|
| | 1 | 2 | 3 | 4 |
| Total Number of Countries Contributing Troops | .895 | | | |
| Total Spending in US Dollar | .837 | | | |
| Total Number of Military and Police Deployed | .781 | | | |
| Number of Civilian Staff | .744 | | | |
| Mandate of Peacekeeping Operation | .735 | | | |
| Era of Peacekeeping Operation | | | | |
| Duration of Conflict in Days | | .766 | | |
| Number of Days between Start of Conflict and Start of PKO | | .709 | | |
| Total Number of Fatalities in Conflict | | .609 | | |
| Percentage of Great Powers Involved | | -.579 | | |
| Conflict Issue | | | -.566 | |
| Duration of Peacekeeping Operation in Months | | | | |
| Type of Conflict | | | | .713 |
| Region of Peacekeeping Operation | | | | -.570 |

Extraction Method: Principal Component Analysis.

a. 4 components extracted.

*Table 3.4B Pattern Matrix(a)*

Pattern Matrix$^a$

| | Component | | | |
|---|---|---|---|---|
| | 1 | 2 | 3 | 4 |
| Total Spending in US Dollar | .868 | | | |
| Total Number of Military and Police Deployed | .811 | | | |
| Total Number of Countries Contributing Troops | .752 | | | |
| Duration of Peacekeeping Operation in Months | .610 | | | |
| Conflict Issue | .524 | | | |
| Number of Civilian Staff | .515 | | | |
| Duration of Conflict in Days | | .948 | | |
| Number of Days between Start of Conflict and Start of PKO | | .927 | | |
| Total Number of Fatalities in Conflict | | .520 | | |
| Percentage of Great Powers Involved | | | .858 | |
| Era of Peacekeeping Operation | | | .728 | |
| Mandate of Peacekeeping Operation | | | .724 | |
| Type of Conflict | | | | .795 |
| Region of Peacekeeping Operation | | .532 | | -.604 |

Extraction Method: Principal Component Analysis.

Rotation Method: Oblimin with Kaiser Normalization.

*Pattern Matrix*[a]

| | Component | | | |
|---|---|---|---|---|
| | 1 | 2 | 3 | 4 |
| Total Spending in US Dollar | .868 | | | |
| Total Number of Military and Police Deployed | .811 | | | |
| Total Number of Countries Contributing Troops | .752 | | | |
| Duration of Peacekeeping Operation in Months | .610 | | | |
| Conflict Issue | .524 | | | |
| Number of Civilian Staff | .515 | | | |
| Duration of Conflict in Days | | .948 | | |
| Number of Days between Start of Conflict and Start of PKO | | .927 | | |
| Total Number of Fatalities in Conflict | | .520 | | |
| Percentage of Great Powers Involved | | | .858 | |
| Era of Peacekeeping Operation | | | .728 | |
| Mandate of Peacekeeping Operation | | | .724 | |
| Type of Conflict | | | | .795 |
| Region of Peacekeeping Operation | | .532 | | -.604 |

Extraction Method: Principal Component Analysis.

Rotation Method: Oblimin with Kaiser Normalization.

a. Rotation converged in 25 iterations.

Examination of the factor loadings presented in the *Pattern Matrix* reveals that thirteen of the fourteen variables loaded highly on the four factors or components extracted. One variable, *region of peacekeeping operation,* cross-

loaded significantly across *Factor 2* and *Factor 4*. We have decided to ignore
that variable in the interpretation of the results to make the interpretation easier.

*Table 3.4C Structure Matrix*

Structure Matrix

| | Component | | | |
|---|---|---|---|---|
| | 1 | 2 | 3 | 4 |
| Total Spending in US Dollar | .897 | | | |
| Total Number of Military and Police Deployed | .827 | | | |
| Total Number of Countries Contributing Troops | .819 | | | |
| Number of Civilian Staff | .590 | | | |
| Duration of Peacekeeping Operation in Months | .541 | | | |
| Conflict Issue | .505 | | | |
| Duration of Conflict in Days | | .940 | | |
| Number of Days between Start of Conflict and Start of PKO | | .904 | | |
| Total Number of Fatalities in Conflict | | .548 | | |
| Percentage of Great Powers Involved | | | .860 | |
| Mandate of Peacekeeping Operation | | | .759 | |
| Era of Peacekeeping Operation | | | .735 | |
| Type of Conflict | | | | .799 |
| Region of Peacekeeping Operation | | .539 | | -.591 |

Extraction Method: Principal Component Analysis.

Rotation Method: Oblimin with Kaiser Normalization.

The *Scree Plot* displayed below helps to graphically determine the optimal number of components. From this Scree Plot, it clearly appears that the *four-factor model* is sufficient to represent our observed data on UN peacekeeping operations. The eigenvalue of each component in the initial solution is plotted. Generally, one wants to extract the components on the steep slope. The components on the shallow slope contribute little to the solution. The last big drop occurs between the fourth and fifth components. So, using the first four components was an easy choice (see Figure 3.1). Robert Ho's explanation of the Scree Plot is quite accurate and helps the reader better understand *Figure 3.1.*:

> The scree test is derived by plotting the eigenvalues (on the Y axis) against the number of factors in their order of extraction (on the X axis). The initial factors extracted are large factors (with high eigenvalues), followed by smaller factors. Graphically, the plot will show a steep slope between the large factors and the gradual trailing off of the rest of the factors. The point at which the curve first begins to straighten out is considered to indicate the maximum number of factors to extract. That is, those factors above this point of inflection are deemed meaningful, and those below are not. (2006, 205)

*Figure 3.1: Optimal Number of Components*

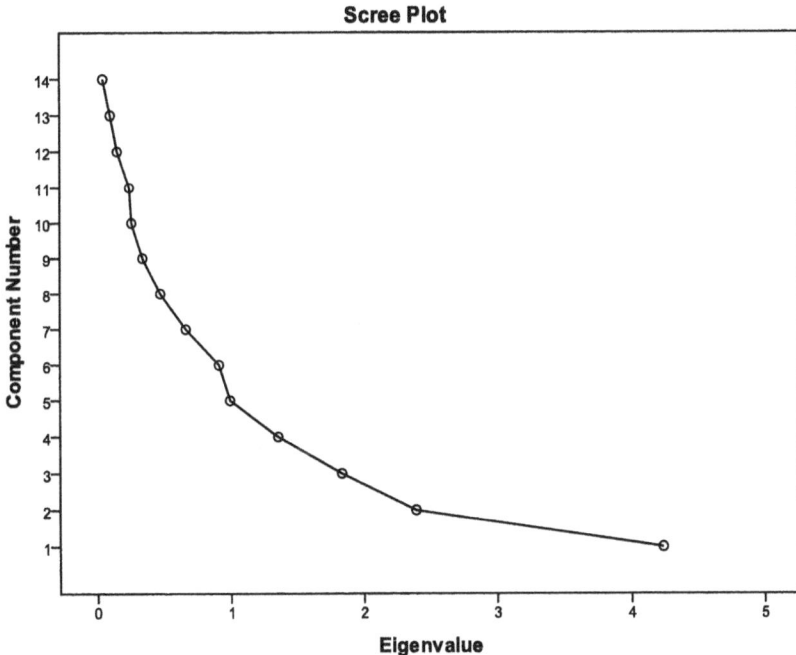

## Endnotes

---

1. This chapter lays out the statistical analytic design and describes the procedures used in the conduct of this study. The development of the chapter reminds the reader that the ultimate purpose of the study is to conduct an empirically grounded research which helps to make meaningful predictions of important factors that may affect the outcome of UN peacekeeping. The chapter is made of tables resulting from the data analysis, using selected quantitative analytic methods.

2. The analysis has sorted the rotated factor pattern in order to facilitate the interpretation of the factors. As a result, the variables with small factor loadings are suppressed and those with large loadings appear together. For the purpose of this study, the analysis has requested that only loadings that are higher than 0.5 in absolute value on a given factor are displayed for the very variables.

# Chapter 4

# Interpretation of the Statistical Results, and Implications for Theory, Policymaking and Research

The previous chapter has described the statistical procedures used in this study, with the results of the analysis. This chapter interprets the quantitative estimation results obtained through the use of factor analysis. The chapter also discusses the major findings from the study and their implications for theory, policymaking and research. In that process, the authors underline the limitations of this study and make suggestions and recommendations for future research.[i]

## Interpretation of the Results

As stated earlier, the four factors retained do explain more than 70% of the variance in the factor analytic model, thereby suggesting that the 14 original variables are well represented.

The first factor is associated with the following six variables: *TOSPEND (Total Spending in US$,* loaded '.868'), *NUMIPO (Total Number of Military and Police Personnel Deployed,* loaded '.811'), *NUCOCO (Total Number of Countries Contributing Troops,* loaded '.752'), *PKODUR (Duration of Peacekeeping Operation,* loaded '.610'), CONIS *(Conflict Issue,* loaded '.524'), and *NUCIST (Number of Civilian Staff,* loaded '.515'). Because the loadings on each variable reflect its relative significance for the factor considered, we note that the *Total Spending in US$ (.868)* is (or may be) more important to the success of a UNPKO than the *Total Number of Military and Police Deployed (.811),* than *Total Number of Countries Contributing Troops (.752),* than *Duration of Peacekeeping Operation (.610),* than *Conflict Issue (.524),* and than the *Number of Civilian Staff (.515),* respectively. We may also infer from these statistics that the *Total Spending in US$* matters, especially if it is spent on uniformed personnel on the ground. However, it seems most appropriate to conclude that this factor indicates that the larger the amount of human and financial resources used, and the more time invested in a UN peacekeeping operation, the more likely that operation is to succeed. In addition, this factor indicates that the UNPKOs deployed in secession conflicts are more likely to last longer and have a higher probability of success than operations deployed in conflicts that do not involve secession issues. In other words, each one of these variables, taken in isolation, constitutes a necessary, but not a sufficient condition for UNPKO success. All six variables must work in interaction for success in UN peacekeeping to take place. Sufficient funding and time must be matched with large numbers of military and police and civilian staff for successful UN peacekeeping operations. These six variables have in common the fact that they mainly revolve around the resources invested in UN peacekeeping operation in terms of the amount money, uniformed and civil personnel, and the amount of time. They constitute the resources component of UNPKOs. Therefore, the factor may be labeled as the *scope of resources invested in peacekeeping factor (F1)*. According to *Table 3.3*, this factor (F1) explains more than 30% of the total variance in the model.

The second factor is associated with the following four variables: *CONDUR (conflict duration*, loaded '.948'), *PKOTIME (number of days spent between the start of the conflict hostilities and the start/deployment of the peacekeeping operation*, loaded '.927'), *TONUFA (total number of fatalities registered in the conflict*, loaded '.520'), and *PKORE (region of peacekeeping operation*, loaded '.532'). However, because *PKORE* cross-loaded across Factor 2 and Factor 4, we have decided to ignore that variable in our interpretation. As a result, the second factor is formed by the three variables *CONDUR*, *PKOTIME*, and *TONUFA*. The first variable indicates the time spent between the start of hostilities and the moment when the conflict is considered settled or resolved. The second variable represents the amount of time spent observing the dynamics of the conflict and making preparations for the deployment of the peacekeeping intervention. The third variable represents the level of intensity of the conflict. The loadings for each variable suggest their relative order of significance for the factor considered. We note that the *duration of the conflict in days (.948)* is more important than the *number of days between the start of conflict hostilities and the start of the peacekeeping operation (.927)*, and than the *total number of fatalities in conflict (.520)*. Because of the relatively low loading of *TONUFA (.520)* in comparison with the high loadings of *CONDUR (.948)* and *PKOTIME (.927)*, the analyst might conclude that this factor is almost absorbed in the variables of *CONDUR* and *PKOTIME*. Yet, the loading of *TONUFA* is relevant to our interpretation of the factor. Indeed, in the presence of *TONUFA*, this factor supports the findings by Jackson (1952) and Young (1967) that the higher the number of fatalities in conflict, the higher the chances of a successful intervention. But it contradicts the long-held belief among scholars that higher casualties in conflict increase the likelihood of unsuccessful intervention (Regan 1996; Bercovitch et al. 1991; Brokner 1982; Burton 1969; Modelski 1964).

What is most important, however, is that this factor indicates that the longer a conflict lasts, and the more the UN waits and prepares before intervening, the more likely the peacekeeping operation to succeed. This finding seems to support Northedge and Dolan's suggestion that mediation is successful only when a conflict has lasted over a period (Northedge and Dolan 1971). However, it sharply contrasts with the claim made by many other international conflict management scholars that early intervention in conflicts yields a higher probability of success (Doyle and Sambanis 2006; Edmead 1971; Bercovitch et al. 1991). Doyle and Sambanis (2006) find that "peace interventions must happen quickly, if they are to be successful" because "early interventions pay more than late ones" (p.132).

This factor may be labeled *F2*: *the duration and intensity of conflict and time of preparation for peacekeeping intervention.* According to *Table 3.3*, *F2* accounts for more than 17% of the variance in our *determinants of UNPKO success* factor analytic model.

The third factor is associated with the following three variables: *Percentage of Great Powers Involved (PEGREP,* loaded '.858'), *Era of Peacekeeping Operation (PKERA,* loaded '.728'), and *Mandate of Peacekeeping Operation (PKOMAN,* loaded '.724').* These three variables revolve essentially around the political support for peacekeeping from the UN Security Council. As a result, we have termed this factor as the *political support to peacekeeping from the UN Security Council* factor, *F3.* This factor seems to suggest that the end of the Cold War has made it possible to increase the percentage of great power involvement, and to achieve more integrated (broader scope) mandates, thereby fostering more success in UN peacekeeping operations than during the Cold War era. The probability of success for peacekeeping operations that occurred during the *post-Cold War era* –coded *(2)* is higher than for those deployed during the *Cold War era* –coded *(1)* because the break-up of the Soviet Union has affected decision-making in international politics in ways that differ from policymaking initiatives and orientations in the bipolar world. *F3* explains more than 13% of the variance in our *determinants of UNPKO success* factor analytic model. Because the loadings on each variable reflect its relative significance for the factor considered, we note that the *Percentage of Great Powers Involved (.858)* is (or may be) more important to the success of a UNPKO than the *Era of Peacekeeping Operation (.728)* and the *Mandate of Peacekeeping Operation (.724),* respectively. We may also infer from these statistics that *Era of Peacekeeping Operation* matters. As we have mentioned above, it seems most appropriate to conclude that the end of the Cold War has indeed made it possible to increase the percentage of great power involvement, and to achieve more integrated mandates, thereby fostering more success in UN peacekeeping operations than during the Cold War era. In other words, each one of these variables, taken in isolation, constitutes a necessary, but not a sufficient condition for UNPKO success. All three variables must work in interaction for success in UN peacekeeping to take place.

The fourth factor comprises the following two variables: *Type of Conflict (CONTYPE,* loaded '.795'), and *Region of Peacekeeping Operation (PKORE,* loaded '-.604'). However, because *PKORE* cross-loaded across *Factor 2* and *Factor 4,* we have decided to ignore that variable in our interpretation. As a result, the fourth factor is merely absorbed by the variable, *CONTYPE* (Type of Conflict, loaded '.795'). In light of that information, the analysis frames *F4* in the categories of *Type of Conflict.* Keeping in mind the logic backing our coding system where the numbers are measures of increasing significance, this result suggests that there is a higher likelihood of success for UN peacekeeping operations in interstate than in intrastate conflict. This factor (F4) explains nearly 10% of the total variance in the model, according to *Table 3.3*.

In sum, using a principal axis factors extraction, the analysis uncovered four underlying factors relating to four categories of measured independent variables. The four factors are, by order of decreasing importance: i) the *scope of resources invested in peacekeeping*; ii) the *duration and intensity of conflict and time of preparation for peacekeeping intervention*; iii) the *political support for peacekeeping from the UN Security Council*; and iv) the *type of conflict*.

These explanatory factors account for more than 70% of the variance in our factor analytic model. The four factors highlight characteristics of both conflict and UN peacekeeping operations. Five of the six variables that constitute the first factor are characteristics of UN peacekeeping operations (*Total Spending in US$, Total Number of Military and Police Deployed, Total Number of Countries Contributing Troops, Duration of Peacekeeping Operation*, and *Number of Civilian Staff*), and one is a characteristic of conflict (*Conflict Issue*). The three variables composing the second factor all represent characteristics of conflict (*Duration of conflict, Number of Days between Start of Conflict and Start of PKO, Total Number of Fatalities in Conflict*). The third factor is made of three variables, all characteristics of UN peacekeeping operations (*Percentage of Great Powers Involved in Peacekeeping, Era of Peacekeeping*, and *Mandate of Peacekeeping*). The fourth factor consists of one characteristic of conflict (*Type of Conflict*). Overall, the four factors enhance eight characteristics of UN peacekeeping (or nine if we count the variable, *region of peacekeeping*, that cross-loaded across *Factor 2* and *Factor 4*), and five characteristics of conflict. This suggests that though the UN might not be able to change much about the characteristics of conflict, it can certainly do something about the characteristics of its peacekeeping operations in order to raise their chances of success. In other words, what seems to matter the most are the UN peacekeeping operations and how they are planned and conducted.

The result of this study yields strong evidence in support of our hypothesis *(H)*: The characteristics of UN peacekeeping and its outcome can be explained by a small number of factors that relate to four categories of measured variables.

The following section describes the implications and limitations of the study.

# Implications for Research and Policy and Limitations of the Study

This section discusses the implications of the major findings for the theory and practice of UN peacekeeping operations, and makes suggestions for policymaking and research. The section is a reflection upon the completed research. It is divided in two parts. The first one describes some of the contributions that the study makes to peacekeeping research and practice and the implications for policymaking. The second one discusses the limitations of the study in light of the findings and lays out some recommendations for future research and policymaking on peacekeeping.

# Contribution to Peacekeeping Research and Practice and Implications for Policymaking

This study represents a major contribution to systematic quantitative research on peacekeeping as it covers a large $N$ of peacekeeping operations ($N = 46$) to examine the determinants of success in UN peacekeeping operations. The need to gather generalizable information has been a challenge for research on peacekeeping. A considerable amount of peacekeeping research has adopted the case study approach (e.g., Boutros-Ghali 1995; Miall, Ramsbotham and Woodhouse 1999; Berman and Sams 2000; Laremont 2002; MacQueen 2002; Adebajo 2004; Durch 2004; Bellamy, Williams, and Griffin 2005). By providing a systematic approach to studying the characteristics of peacekeeping and the factors that affect peacekeeping outcomes, this research offers an original and useful model for evaluating UN peacekeeping operations. Applying the literature on conflict management to peacekeeping, and using principal component analysis, the study suggests an original approach to conduct empirical research on peacekeeping within a theoretical framework, by focusing on a few characteristics of UN peacekeeping operations and armed conflicts to identify a small number of factors that determine success in UN peacekeeping operations.

The core contribution of this study to peacekeeping research is that the principal component analysis has uncovered four factors which account for more than 70% of the variability among the variables characterizing UN peacekeeping operations and armed conflicts. The four factors are: : (1) the *scope of resources invested in peacekeeping*; (2) the *duration and intensity of conflict and time of preparation for peacekeeping intervention*; (3) the *political support for peacekeeping from the UN Security Council*; and (4) the *type of conflict*. Those four factors suggest various patterns of contributors that interact for success in UN peacekeeping.

One lesson that policymakers can learn from this work on peacekeeping is that it gives hope in terms of what they should focus on in peacekeeping policymaking. They should focus on the four factors we have identified. Specifically, the findings suggest that policymakers ought to concentrate more on the characteristics of the peacekeeping operations, i.e. the importance of taking enough time to prepare and design a peacekeeping operation and putting sufficient resources into the process of conducting the operation, rather than on the characteristics of the armed conflicts. The implication here is twofold, that the UN should (1) avoid emotional calls for intervention at the early stage of conflict and (2) invest sufficient resources (human and financial, as well as time) into peacekeeping operations. Doing so increases the chances of success in UN peacekeeping. In other words, the first factor, *F1*, implies that the success of a UN peacekeeping operation depends (at a varying degree as reflected by the variables loadings in the *Pattern Matrix – Table 3.4B*) on how much money the international community invests in that peacekeeping operation, how many uniformed personnel and civilian staff are deployed, and how long is the peacekeeping operation: the more money the UN spends on a higher number of uniformed personnel and civilian staff deployed in a peacekeeping operation that lasts over a long period of time, the more likely the operation is to succeed.

Another lesson this study implies for policymaking is that each peacekeeping operation should be designed to meet specific needs of specific situations, depending on the type of conflict, the conflict issue, the duration of conflict and the number of fatalities in conflict. Regarding the duration of conflict and the number of casualties, the second factor $(F2)$ tells us that the longer a conflict lasts, the more fatalities it creates, and the more the UN waits and prepares before intervening, the more likely the peacekeeping operation to succeed. A successful UN peacekeeping requires enough time for preparation. A long preparation time allows the UN to become familiar with the issues, the parties (or stakeholders), and dynamics of the conflict in order to gather adequate means and design the right strategies to intervene successfully. It is critically important to take time to get to know and understand a conflict sufficiently before intervention for the sake of effectiveness. As far as the issues of conflict are concerned, the first factor $(F1)$ is also explicit: UN peacekeeping operations that address conflicts over secession issues are more likely to be longer and have greater chances of success than UN peacekeeping operations addressing conflicts that have nothing to do with secession issues. Regarding the type of conflict, the fourth factor, $F4$, shows us that there is a higher probability of success for UN peacekeeping operations in interstate than in intrastate conflict. Based on the results here, it is impossible to create a single pattern of peacekeeping operation that can be replicated successfully in every situation of armed conflicts. Each divided society, each war-torn nation, and each conflict-shattered region have their needs and requirements. As a result, each peacekeeping mission should be designed accordingly. In this regard Doyle and Sambanis (2006) suggest that each mission must be designed to meet the needs of a particular conflict, with adequate resources.

A final and more important lesson for policymakers is that political support for peacekeeping operations can boost the chances of successful UN peacekeeping operations. Political support for peacekeeping is expressed through broader mandates and the involvement of the five permanent members of the Security Council (France, Russia, China, the United Kingdom, and the United States) in contributing troops for peacekeeping. The third factor $(F3)$ suggests that peacekeeping operations with multidimensional mandates are more likely to result in successful outcomes.

## Limitations of the Study and Final Recommendations

It is fair to acknowledge there are a few limitations to this study. These limitations appeal to future research in this area to expand the scope of variables characterizing peacekeeping operations and armed conflicts.

First, critics of this work may consider the fact that the study did not completely rely on standard data sources for empirical research on war as a limitation to this work. As we have indicated previously, the analyst could anticipate that the results of this study might be different if it were to rely upon the databases of armed conflicts provided by the *Correlates of War Project* (1982) or by *UCDP/PRIO Armed Conflict Dataset* (2002) due to differences in coding and variables operationalization.

Second, the study did not take into account the variable of the *previous relationship between the conflicting parties*. Scholars of conflict management found that conditions relating to the nature of the relationship between the conflicting parties affect success in mediation (Bercovitch et al., 1991). This could also apply to success in peacekeeping: it could be significant that the characteristics of the parties in terms of the nature of their *previous relationships (friendship or constant antagonism)* determine peacekeeping outcome. We were not able to verify this due to issues of missing data. Given the important roles of the disputants in most successful conflict management processes, one can suggest that success in peacekeeping might not be if the conflicting parties are not willing to work for peace. Eventually, success or failure in UN peacekeeping could be mainly a function of the parties' good will, as it is for success or failure in conflict management (Jackson 2000).[ii]

Third, this study did not consider variables of culture and leadership skills found in qualitative studies on peacekeeping. Future quantitative research will need to include cultural factors and leadership qualities of the special representatives of the UN Secretary General and senior officers that pilot peacekeeping operations to test their significance for successful peacekeeping operations.

Based on the qualitative literature, other factors that contribute to successful peacekeeping include cultural dimensions (Rubinstein 2008), the composition of the peacekeeping mission and its affinity to the culture or ethnic identity of the conflicting parties, the characteristic of the leadership of the peacekeeping mission, distributive versus integrative processes, primary or third-party roles, as well as the goal-setting, the situation analysis, the tactics or strategy used in the peacekeepers' decision-making (see Wall, Druckman, and Diehl 2002, Adebajo 2004).

Rubinstein (2008) suggests that cultural elements and considerations affect peacekeeping outcome significantly. He argues that culture impacts interactions between peacekeeping forces and local populations, peacekeepers and NGOs in host countries, as well as mission planning and the deployment of troops. His perspective enhances the criticality of culture to peacekeeping success or failure. Some works on peacekeeping highlight that the composition of peacekeeping contingents should avoid cultural and linguistic differences among the peacekeepers because such differences are not conducive to peacekeeping effectiveness. Proponents of this position include Ahlquist (1996), Elron (1999), and Duffey (2000). These scholars argue that linguistic and cultural differences (or even limitations) result in sharp misrepresentations, miscommunications, misunderstanding, disagreements and lacks of collaboration, which reduce the chances for success in peacekeeping.

A few peacekeeping scholars emphasize the function of ethnic or cultural affinity between a peacekeeping mission and the parties to the conflict. The proponents include Diehl (1994) and Duffey (2000). For instance, Tamara Duffey associates success in peacekeeping with the maintenance by the peacekeeping forces of good relations with the local community and the "peacekeepers' understanding of the local population's culture and respect for their cultural traditions" (Duffey 2000, p. 150). Diehl suggests that the probability of success for a peacekeeping mission is high if the peacekeepers come from the same region where conflict unfolds, on the ground that ethnic or cultural affinity fosters trust and legitimacy, while non-affinity fosters a lack of trust and illegitimacy (Diehl 1994). Because language is a cultural vehicle, cultural affinity encompasses the ability to understand and speak the language of local populations and the mission language. The *Brahimi Report* on peacekeeping suggests that some missions fail because of the inability of some peacekeepers to speak the mission language (Brahimi 2000, p. 8).

Critics might still argue here that operating on the basis of cultural or ethnic similarities between peacekeepers and conflicting parties holds risks of biases or partiality for the peacekeeping mission: some peacekeepers might be partial by siding with the parties belonging to (or close to) their ethnic or cultural group.

Without emphasizing cultural or ethnic affinities, other scholars stress the importance for the peacekeepers to understand the local culture of the peacekeeping environment for a successful mission. This group of scholars includes Wall, Druckman, and Diehl (2002) as well as Rubinstein (2008). According to them, peacekeepers are faced with a number of cultural obstacles they need to be aware of and adjust to for a successful mission. The first obstacle for military personnel is that of a civilian culture. Whereas peacekeeping troops fit in a military culture where getting orders and obeying represent the norms, civilians belong to a different culture and "do not like being ordered about, especially by military personnel" (Wall, Druckman, and Diehl 2002, p. 153). The impact of these cultural differences translates into differences in goals between military and civilian, which result in civilians disliking or distrusting soldiers. Military peacekeepers ought to be aware of such cultural differences and embrace the civilian worldview in the environment where they are posted. The second obstacle is that of the indigenous culture which perceives conflict differently and has different social structures with different norms regarding interpersonal relations. Here as well, peacekeepers ought to be mindful of those differences in order to control or adjust their behavior for the sake of a successful mission.

The quality of the mission leadership is also an important factor that may affect peacekeeping outcome. Some peacekeeping scholars argue that the provision of good leadership, especially as the head of mission, represents a factor that contributes to successful peacekeeping (Adebajo 2004). As a result, a head of mission with credentials and skills for facilitation, negotiation, mediation, and coordination matched with a sense of integrity and cultural adjustment is likely to increase the chances of success of the mission of which he or she is in charge. The *Brahimi Report* concurs when it stresses that "the tenor of an entire mission can be heavily influenced by the character and ability of those who lead it" simply because "effective, dynamic leadership can make the difference between a cohesive mission with high morale and effectiveness despite adverse circumstances, and one that struggles to maintain any of those attributes" (Brahimi 2000, p. 92). This assumes, quite naively, that leadership capabilities are not dependent on the context or environment in which it is exercised. We need to take a contingency approach here. A good leader in a given context may be very bad in a different context.

Among other factors that may influence peacekeeping outcome, scholars underline distributive versus integrative processes, primary or third-party roles, as well as the goal-setting, the situation analysis, the tactics or strategy used in the peacekeepers' decision-making (see Wall, Druckman, and Diehl 2002; Adebajo 2004). Wall, Druckman, and Diehl argue that in an integrative process, the peacekeeping forces adopt a problem-solving approach which addresses the root causes of the conflict, whereas they take a settlement approach in a distributive approach with the concern of having the parties reach an agreement. It is suggested that an integrative process might be more likely to bear a successful outcome than a distributive process.[iii] Success might also depend on whether the peacekeepers play primary or third-party roles. Primary-party roles involve the peacekeepers controlling or modifying the behavior of the other parties to the conflict, whereas third-party missions require that the peacekeepers control the relationships between the disputants (Wall, Druckman, and Diehl 2002, p.158). Moreover, success might depend on whether the peacekeepers set short-term or long-term goals that take into consideration the goals of all parties involved, or on their analytical assets, or on the tactics or strategy they utilize during the operation. "Peacekeepers can set a goal of maximizing their own outcomes and those accruing to their constituency. Or they may ignore the concrete, short-term outcomes to concentrate upon improvement of the relationships among the parties" (Wall, Druckman, and Diehl 2002, p. 146). In addition, the peacekeepers should resort to good analytical skills to identify and understand the causes of the conflict in order to use appropriate tactics and strategy to address them adequately and successfully (Wall, Druckman, and Diehl 2002).

All the limitations of this study show the need for more systematic quantitative/empirical research on peacekeeping. It can be inferred from the findings and their implications that this study shows the need to develop more sophisticated measurements and to expand the scope of variables characterizing armed conflicts and UN peacekeeping operations, which ultimately is our first recommendation for future research. Our second recommendation for future research is to investigate larger numbers of peacekeeping operations over larger periods.

**Endnotes**

---

1. This chapter provides interpretations of the results obtained from the data analysis to identify which factors determine success in UN peacekeeping and to what extent. The reader should keep in mind that the statistical tests were performed on an original dataset over a temporal domain of 1956-2006, and a spatial domain that encompasses 46 UN peacekeeping operations. In its final section, the chapter presents the implications of the findings for research and policy as well as the limitations of the study.

2. Note that there may be a significant difference between Non-UN or even UN ad hoc conflict mediation initiatives, which may depend essentially on the parties' goodwill for success, and UNPKOs that carry at least a minimum amount of constraint on the part of the UN.

3. Note that processes are not distributive or integrative *per se*, but can be categorized as such as a result of the observed reality of the relationships between the parties.

# References

Adebajo, Adekeye. 2004. From Congo to Congo: United Nations Peacekeeping in Africa after the Cold War. In *Africa in international politics: External involvement on the continent,* ed. Ian Taylor and Paul Williams, 195-212. London and New York: Routledge.

Ahlquist, Leif. 1996. *Co-operation, command and control in UN peace-keeping operations.* Department of Operational Studies, National Defence College of Sweden.

Babbie, Earl. 2004. *The practice of social research.* Belmont, CA: Wadsworth/Thomson Learning.

Balencie, Jean-Marc, and Arnaud Grange (de La). 1999. *Mondes rebelles: Guerres civiles et violences politiques.* Paris: Editions Michalon.

Barros, James. 1970. *The League of Nations and the great powers: The Greek-Bulgarian incident 1925.* Oxford: Oxford University Press.

Bellamy, Alex J., Paul Williams, and Stuart Griffin. 2004. *Understanding peacekeeping.* Cambridge: Polity Press.

Bennett, LeRoy A. 1984. *International organizations: principles and issues.* 3$^{rd}$ ed. London: Prentice Hall.

Bercovitch, Jacob. 1991. International mediation and dispute settlement: Evaluating the conditions for successful mediation. *Negotiation Journal* 7 (1): 17-30.

Bercovitch, Jacob, Theodore J. Anagnoson, and Donnette L. Wille. 1991. Some conceptual issues and empirical trends in the study of successful mediation in international relations. *Journal of Peace Research* 28(1): 7-17.

Bercovitch, Jacob, and Judith Fretter. 2004. *Regional guide to international conflict and management from 1945 to 2003.* Washington, DC: CQ Press.

Bercovitch, Jacob, and Allison Houston. 1993. Influence of mediator characteristics and behaviour on the success of mediation in international relations. *International Journal of Conflict Management* 4(4): 297-321.

Bercovitch, Jacob, and Allison Houston. 1996. The study of international mediation: theoretical issues and empirical evidence, in *Resolving international conflict: The theory and practice of mediation,* ed. Jacob Bercovitch, 11-35. Boulder, CO: Lynne Rienner.

Bercovitch, Jacob, and Richard Jackson. 1997. *International conflict: A chronological encyclopedia of conflicts and their management 1945-1995.* Washington, DC: Washington Quarterly.

Bercovitch, Jacob, and J. Lamare. 1993. The process of international mediation: An analysis of the determinants of successful and unsuccessful outcomes. *Australian Journal of Political Science* 28: 290-305.

Bercovitch, Jacob, ed. 2002. *Studies in international mediation.* New York: Palgrave Macmillan.

Bercovitch, Jacob, and J. Langley. 1993. The nature of the dispute and the effectiveness of international mediation. The *Journal of Conflict Resolution* 37:670-691.

Berdal, Mats R. 1993. *Whither UN peacekeeping?* London: Adelphi Paper no. 281, Oxford University Press for the IISS.

Berman, Eric G., and Katie E. Sams. 2000. *Peacekeeping in Africa: Capabilities and culpabilities.* Geneva: United Nations Institute for Disarmament Research.

Boulding, Kenneth E. 1990. *Three faces of power.* Newbury Park, CA: Sage Publications.

Boutros-Ghali, Boutros 1995. *An agenda for peace.* 2<sup>nd</sup> Edition. New York: United Nations.

Bratt, Duane. 1996. Assessing the success of UN peacekeeping operations. *International Peacekeeping* 3: 64-81.

Brown, A. M. 1993. "United Nations peacekeeping: Historical overview and current issues", Report for Congress (Washington, D.C.: Congressional Research Service).

Burton, John W. 1987. *Resolving deep-rooted conflict: A handbook.* Lanham, MD: University Press of America.

Bush, Robert Baruch A., and Joseph P. Folger. 1994. *The promise of mediation: Responding to conflict through empowerment and recognition.* San Francisco: Jossey-Bass Inc.

Buzan, Barry, and Richard Little. 2000. *International systems in world history: Remaking the study of international relations.* Oxford: Oxford University Press

Carnahan, M., W. Durch, and S. Gilmore. 2006. *Economic impact of peacekeeping.* New York: United Nations Peacekeeping Best Practice Unit.

Carter, Neal, and Sean Byrne. 2000. The dynamics of social cubism: A view from Northern Ireland and Quebec. In *Reconcilable differences: Turning points in ethnopolitical conflict,* ed. Sean Byrne and Cynthia L. Irvin, 41-62. West Hartford, CT: Kumarian Press.

Claude, Inis. 1963. *Swords into Ploughshares: the Problems and Progress of International Organization.* 4<sup>th</sup> ed. New York: McGraw Hill.

Costantino, Cathy A., and Christina S. Merchant. 1996. *Designing conflict management systems: A guide to creating productive and healthy organizations.* San Francisco: Jossey-Bass Inc., Publishers.

Diehl, Paul F. (1994). *International peacekeeping.* Revised edition. Baltimore, MD: John Hopkins University Press.

Diehl, Paul F., Daniel Druckman, and James Wall. 1998. International peacekeeping and conflict resolution: A taxonomic analysis with implications. *Journal of Conflict Resolution* 42:33-55.

Doyle, Michael, Ian Johnstone, and Robert C. Orr, eds. 1997. *Keeping the peace: lessons from multidimensional UN operations in Cambodia and El Salvador.* Cambridge: Cambridge University Press.

Doyle, Michael, and Nicholas Sambanis. 2006. *Making war and building peace: United Nations peace operations.* Princeton: Princeton University Press.

Downes, John, and Jordan E. Goodman. 2007. *Dictionary of finance and investment terms* (7th Edition). New York: Baron's Educational Series.

Druckman, Daniel, and Paul C. Stern. 1997. Evaluating peacekeeping missions. *Mershon International Studies Review* 41: 151-165.

Duffey, Tamara. 2000. Cultural issues in UN peacekeeping. *International Peacekeeping* 7: 142-166.

Durch, William, ed. 1993. *The evolution of UN peacekeeping: case studies and comparative analysis.* New York: St. Martin's Press.

Durch, William. 1996. *UN peacekeeping, American policy, and the uncivil wars of the 1990s.* New York: St. Martin's Press.

Edmead, Frank. 1971. *Analysis and prediction in international mediation.* London: Unitar.

Elron, Efrat, Boas Shamir, and Eyal Ben-Ari. 1999. Why don't they fight each other? Cultural diversity and operational unity in multinational forces. *Armed Forces and Society,* 26:73-91.

Essis, Essoh J. M.C. 1997. *State preferences in multilateral nuclear non-proliferation policy-making: An empirical analysis of the 1995 NPT review and extension conference*. Ph.D. dissertation, George Mason University

Evans, Gareth. 1993. *Cooperating for Peace: The Global agenda for the 1990s and beyond*. St. Leonard's, New South Wales: Allen and Unwin.

Fetherston, A. B. 1994. *Towards a theory of United Nations peacekeeping*. New York: St. Martin's Press.

Fetherston, A. B. 1995. Habitus in cooperating for peace: A critique of peacekeeping. In *The new agenda for global security: Cooperating for peace and beyond*, ed. Stephanie Lawson. St. Leonards, New South Wales: Allen and Unwin.

Fisher, Ronald. 1995. Pacific, impartial third-party intervention in international conflict: A review analysis. In *Beyond confrontation: Learning conflict resolution in the post-Cold War era*, ed. John A. Vasquez, James T. Johnson, Sanford M. Jaffe, and Linda Stamato, 39-59. Ann Arbor, MI: University of Michigan Press.

Fortna, Virginia. P. 2004. *Peace time: Cease-fire agreements and the durability of peace*. Princeton: Princeton University Press.

Gilligan, M., and S. Stedman. 2003. Where do peacekeepers go? *International Studies Review* 5: 37-54.

Gleditsch, Nils P., Peter Wallensteen, Mikael Erickson, Margareta Sollenberg, and Harvard Strand. 2002. 'Armed conflict 1946-2001: A new dataset'. *Journal of Peace Research* 39(5): 615-637.

Goulding, Marrack. 1996. The use of force by the United Nations. *International Peacekeeping* 3 (1): 1-18.

Greig, Michael J., and Paul F. Diehl. 2005. The peacekeeping-peacemaking dilemma. *International Studies Quarterly* 49: 621-645.

Hansen, A. S. 2000. International security assistance to war-torn societies. In *Regeneration of war-torn societies*, ed. Michael Pugh, 35-53. London: Macmillan.

Harman, Harry H. 1967. *Modern factor analysis*. Second Edition Revised. Chicago: The University of Chicago Press.

Harff, Barbara, and Gurr, Ted R. 2004. *Ethnic conflict in world politics*. Boulder, CO: Westview Press.

HMSO. 1995. *Wider peacekeeping*. London: Ministry of Defence.

Ho, Robert. 2006. *Handbook of univariate and multivariate data analysis and interpretation with SPSS*. Boca Raton, FL: Chapman & Hall/CRC.

Hocker, Joyce L., and Wilmot, William W. 1991. *Interpersonal conflict*. Dubuque. Iowa: William C. Brown

Holm, Tor. T., and Eide, Espen. B., ed. 2000. *Peacebuilding and police reform*. London: Frank Cass.

Hoover, Kenneth R., and Donovan, Todd. 2004. *The elements of social scientific thinking*. Belmont, CA: Wadsworth.

Huntington, Samuel P. 1996. *The clash of civilizations and the remaking of world order*. New York: Simon & Schuster.

Ikenberry, John G. 2001. *After victory: Institutions, strategic restraint, and the rebuilding of order after major wars*. Princeton: Princeton University Press

Jackson, Richard. 2000. Successful negotiation in international violent conflict. *Journal of Peace Research* 37(3): 323-343.

James, Alan. 1990. *Peacekeeping in international politics*. Basingstoke: Macmillan with the IISS.

Johansen, Robert C. 1994. UN peacekeeping: How should we measure success? *Mershon International Studies Review* 38: 307-310.

Kellas, James G. 1998. *The politics of nationalism and ethnicity.* New York: St. Martin's Press.

Kim, Jae-On, and Mueller, Charles. W. 1978. *Introduction to factor analysis: What it is and how to do it.* Newburry Park, CA: Sage Publications.

Kleiboer, M., and t'Hart, P. 1995. Time to talk? Multiple perspective on timing of international mediation. *Cooperation and conflict* 30 (4): 307-348.

Krasno, Jean, Bradd C. Hayes, and Donald C. Daniel, ed. 2003. *Leveraging for success in United Nations peace operations.* Westport, CT: Praeger Publishers.

Kupchan, Charles A., and Clifford A. Kupchan. 1991. Concerts, collective security and the future of Europe. *International Security,* 16 (1), 23-51.

Lederach, John Paul. 1997. *Building peace: Sustainable reconciliation in divided societies.* Washington, DC: United States Institute of Peace Press.

Lloyd-Jones, R. 1977. Primary trait scoring. In *Evaluating writing: Describing, measuring, judging,* ed. Charles Cooper and Lee Odell, Urbana, Ill.: National Council of Teachers of English.

Mackinlay, John. 1998. Beyond the logjam: a doctrine for complex emergencies, *Small Wars and Insurgencies,* 9 (1): 114-31.

MacQueen, Norrie. 2002. *United Nations peacekeeping in Africa since 1960.* London: Longman.

Mangone, Gerard J. 1954. *A short history of international organization.* New York: McGraw Hill

Miall, Hugh, Ramsbotham, Olivier, and Woodhouse, Tom. 1999. *Contemporary conflict resolution.* Cambridge: Polity

Mill, John S. 1956. *On liberty.* Indianapolis: Bobbs-Merrill.

Moore, Christopher W. 1996. *The mediation process: Practical strategies for resolving conflict.* San Francisco: Jossey-Bass Inc., Publishers.

Neack, Laura. 1995. UN peacekeeping: In the interest of community of self? *Journal of Peace Research* 32: 181-196.

Neufeldt, Victoria, ed. 1997. *Webster's new world college dictionary.* New York: Simon & Schuster Macmillan.

Northedge, F.S., and Michael D. Donelan. 1971. *International disputes: The political aspects.* London: Europa.

Ott, M. C. 1972. Mediation as a method of conflict resolution: Two cases, *International Organizations* 24: 595-618.

Pruitt, Dean G., and Carnevale, Peter J. 1993. *Negotiation in social conflict.* Pacific Grove, CA: Brooks/Cole Publishing Company.

Pruitt, Dean. G., Jeffrey Z. Rubin, and Sung H. Kim. 2004. *Social conflict: Escalation, stalemate, and settlement.* New York: McGraw-Hill Companies.

Raymond, G., and C. Kegley. 1985. Third party mediation and international norms: A test of two models. *Conflict management and peace science,*      9: 33-51.

Ratner, Steven R. 1995. *The new UN peacekeeping: Building peace in lands of conflict after the Cold War.* New York: St. Martin's Press.

Regan, Patrick M. 1996. Conditions of successful third-party intervention in intrastate conflict. *The Journal of Conflict Resolution* 40 (2): 336-359.

Regan, Patrick M. 2002. Third party interventions and the duration of intrastate conflict. *The Journal of Conflict Resolution* 46 (1): 55-73.

Regan, Patrick M., and Allan C. Stam. 2000. In the nick of time: Conflict management, mediation timing, and the duration of interstate disputes. *International Studies Quarterly* 44:239-260.

Rubinstein, Robert A. 2008. *Peacekeeping under fire: Culture and intervention.* Boulder, CO: Paradigm Publishers.

Sambanis, Nicholas. 1999. The United Nations operations in Cyprus: A new look at the peacekeeping-peacemaking relationship. *International peacekeeping* 6(1): 79-108.

Sarooshi, Dan. 2000. *The United Nations and the development of collective security.* Oxford: Oxford University Press.

Singer, David J., and Melvin Small. 1972. *The wages of war 1816-1965: A statistical handbook.* New York: Wiley.

Singer, David J., and Melvin Small. 1994. *Correlates of war project: International and civil war data, 1816-1992.* ICPSR or at www.umich.edu/~cowproj).

Small, Melvin, and David J. Singer. 1982. *Resort to arms: International and civil wars, 1816-1980.* Beverly Hills, CA: Sage Publications

Smith, A., Allan Stam. 2003. Mediation and peacekeeping in a random walk model of civil and interstate war. *International Studies Review* 5:115-135.

Stedman, J. Stephen, and George Downs. 2002. Evaluation issues in peace implementation. In *Ending civil wars: The implementation of peace agreements.*, ed. Stephen J. Stedman, Donald Rothchild, and Elizabeth M. Cousens. Boulder, CO: Lynne Rienner Publishers.

Thakur, Ramesh, and Albrecht Schnabel. 2001. Cascading generations of peacekeeping: across the Mogadishu line to Kosovo and Timor, in *United Nations peacekeeping operations: ad hoc missions, permanent engagement*, ed. R. Thakur and A. Schnabel, 3-25. Tokyo: UN University Press

Touval, Saadia, and William I. Zartman. 1989. Mediation in international conflict. In *Mediation research*, ed. Kenneth Kressel, and Dean C. Pruitt. San Francisco: Jossey-Bass.

United Nations. 1990. *The Blue helmets.* New York: United Nations Department of Public Information.

United Nations. 1945. *Charter of the United Nations.* United Nations.

United Nations. 2005. *Charter of the United Nations and statute of the International Court of Justice.* New York: United Nations Department of Public Information.

United Nations. 2003. *Handbook on United Nations multidimensional peacekeeping operations.* New York: United Nations Department of Peacekeeping Operations.

United Nations. 2000. *Report of the panel on the United Nations peace operations (Brahimi Report).* New York: United Nations.

UN General Assembly Resolution 1000, 5 November 1956.

UN Security Council Resolution, 1997, S/RES/1123.

UNDPKO. http://www.un.org/Depts/dpko/ops.htm (accessed March 9, 2007).

Urquhart, Brian. 1987. United Nations peacekeeping operations and how their role might be enhanced. In *The United Nations and the maintenance of international peace and security*, ed. UNITAR. Lancaster: Martinus Nijhoff.

Urquhart, Brian. 1990. Beyond the sheriff's posse. *Survival* 32: 196-205.

Ury, William. L., Jeanne M. Brett, and Stephen B. Goldberg. 1988. *Getting disputes resolved: Designing systems to cut the costs of conflict.* San Francisco: Jossey-Bass Inc., Publishers.

Valvoord, Barbara E., and Virginia J. Anderson. 1998. *Effective grading: a tool for learning and assessment.* San Francisco: Jossey-Bass Publishers.

Wainhouse, David. 1966. *International peace observation.* Baltimore, MD: Johns Hopkins University Press.

Wall, James, Daniel Druckman, and Paul F. Diehl. 2002. Mediation by international peacekeepers. In *Studies in International Mediation,* ed. Jacob Bercovitch. New York: Palgrave Macmillan.

Woodhouse, Tom, and Ramsbotham, Olivier. eds. 2000. Peacekeeping and conflict resolution. *International Peacekeeping* (Special Issue) 7(1): 1-253.

Zartman, William I. 1985. *Ripe for resolution.* New York: Oxford University Press

Zartman, William I. 2000. Ripeness: The hurting stalemate and beyond. In *International conflict resolution after the cold war,* ed. P. Stern and Daniel Druckman.Washington, DC: National Academy Press.

Zartmann, William I. and Lewis J. Rasmussen, eds. 1997. *Peacemaking in international conflicts: Methods and techniques.* Washington, DC: United States Institute of Peace.

# Appendices

## Appendix A- Computer Output from Data Analysis

*Factor Analysis output*
FACTOR
/VARIABLES PKOMAN NUMIPO NUCIST NUCOCO PEGREP PKODUR
PKERA CONTYPE CONIS TOSPEND TONUFA CONDUR PKOTIME
PKORE
/MISSING LISTWISE
/ANALYSIS PKOMAN NUMIPO NUCIST NUCOCO PEGREP PKODUR
PKERA CONTYPE CONIS TOSPEND TONUFA CONDUR PKOTIME
PKORE
/PRINT INITIAL CORRELATION KMO EXTRACTION ROTATION
/FORMAT SORT BLANK(.5)
/PLOT EIGEN ROTATION
/CRITERIA MINEIGEN(1) ITERATE(25)
/EXTRACTION PC
/CRITERIA ITERATE(25) DELTA(0)
/ROTATION OBLIMIN
/METHOD=CORRELATION.

Note: The method of factor extraction used is *Principal Components Analysis*.

*KMO and Bartlett's Test*

| Kaiser-Meyer-Olkin Measure of Sampling Adequacy. | | .560 |
|---|---|---|
| Bartlett's Test of Sphericity | Approx. Chi-Square | 271.621 |
| | df | 91 |
| | Sig. | .000 |

*Appendices*

*Communalities*

|  | Initial | Extraction |
|---|---|---|
| Mandate of Peacekeeping Operation | 1.000 | .782 |
| Total Number of Military and Police Deployed | 1.000 | .748 |
| Number of Civilian Staff | 1.000 | .645 |
| Total Number of Countries Contributing Troops | 1.000 | .844 |
| Percentage of Great Powers Involved | 1.000 | .779 |
| Duration of Peacekeeping Operation in Months | 1.000 | .427 |
| Era of Peacekeeping Operation | 1.000 | .578 |
| Type of Conflict | 1.000 | .734 |
| Conflict Issue | 1.000 | .487 |
| Total Spending in US Dollar | 1.000 | .834 |
| Total Number of Fatalities in Conflict | 1.000 | .535 |
| Duration of Conflict in Days | 1.000 | .888 |
| Number of Days between Start of Conflict and Start of PKO | 1.000 | .879 |
| Region of Peacekeeping Operation | 1.000 | .663 |

Extraction Method: Principal Component Analysis.

Total Variance Explained

| Component | Initial Eigenvalues | | | Extraction Sums of Squared Loadings | | | Rotation Sums of Squared Loadings[a] |
|---|---|---|---|---|---|---|---|
| | Total | % of Variance | Cumulative % | Total | % of Variance | Cumulative % | Total |
| 1 | 4.238 | 30.270 | 30.270 | 4.238 | 30.270 | 30.270 | 3.458 |
| 2 | 2.395 | 17.105 | 47.375 | 2.395 | 17.105 | 47.375 | 2.723 |
| 3 | 1.833 | 13.094 | 60.469 | 1.833 | 13.094 | 60.469 | 2.683 |
| 4 | 1.358 | 9.698 | 70.167 | 1.358 | 9.698 | 70.167 | 1.431 |
| 5 | .994 | 7.097 | 77.263 | | | | |
| 6 | .911 | 6.508 | 83.771 | | | | |
| 7 | .664 | 4.745 | 88.516 | | | | |
| 8 | .476 | 3.398 | 91.914 | | | | |
| 9 | .341 | 2.437 | 94.352 | | | | |
| 10 | .257 | 1.836 | 96.188 | | | | |
| 11 | .241 | 1.719 | 97.907 | | | | |
| 12 | .150 | 1.070 | 98.978 | | | | |
| 13 | .099 | .705 | 99.683 | | | | |
| 14 | .044 | .317 | 100.000 | | | | |

Extraction Method: Principal Component Analysis.

a. When components are correlated, sums of squared loadings cannot be added to obtain a total variance.

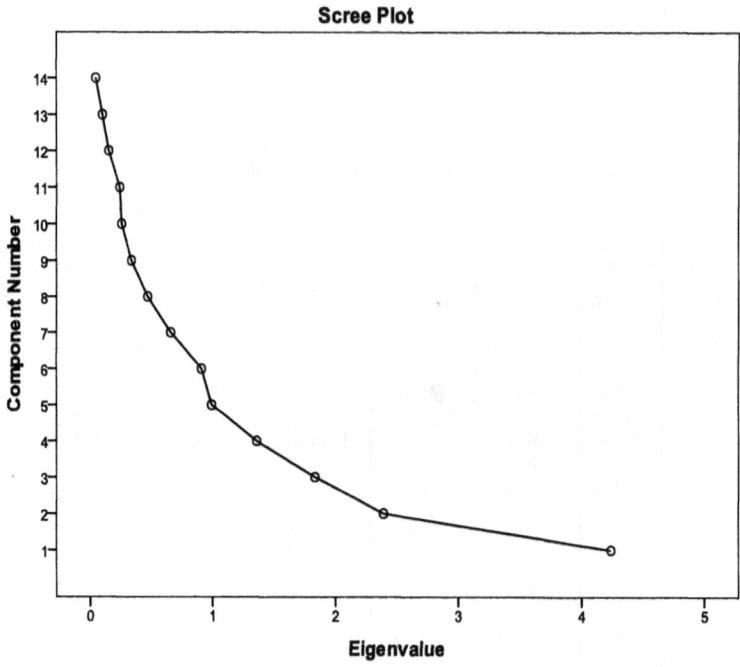

**Scree Plot**

*Component Matrix*[a]

| | Component | | | |
|---|---|---|---|---|
| | 1 | 2 | 3 | 4 |
| Total Number of Countries Contributing Troops | .895 | | | |
| Total Spending in US Dollar | .837 | | | |
| Total Number of Military and Police Deployed | .781 | | | |
| Number of Civilian Staff | .744 | | | |
| Mandate of Peacekeeping Operation | .735 | | | |
| Era of Peacekeeping Operation | | | | |
| Duration of Conflict in Days | | .766 | | |
| Number of Days between Start of Conflict and Start of PKO | | .709 | | |
| Total Number of Fatalities in Conflict | | .609 | | |
| Percentage of Great Powers Involved | | -.579 | | |
| Conflict Issue | | | -.566 | |
| Duration of Peacekeeping Operation in Months | | | | |
| Type of Conflict | | | | .713 |
| Region of Peacekeeping Operation | | | | -.570 |

Extraction Method: Principal Component Analysis.

a. 4 components extracted.

*Pattern Matrix[a]*

|  | Component | | | |
|---|---|---|---|---|
|  | 1 | 2 | 3 | 4 |
| Total Spending in US Dollar | .868 | | | |
| Total Number of Military and Police Deployed | .811 | | | |
| Total Number of Countries Contributing Troops | .752 | | | |
| Duration of Peacekeeping Operation in Months | .610 | | | |
| Conflict Issue | .524 | | | |
| Number of Civilian Staff | .515 | | | |
| Duration of Conflict in Days | | .948 | | |
| Number of Days between Start of Conflict and Start of PKO | | .927 | | |
| Total Number of Fatalities in Conflict | | .520 | | |
| Percentage of Great Powers Involved | | | .858 | |
| Era of Peacekeeping Operation | | | .728 | |
| Mandate of Peacekeeping Operation | | | .724 | |
| Type of Conflict | | | | .795 |
| Region of Peacekeeping Operation | | .532 | | -.604 |

Extraction Method: Principal Component Analysis.

Rotation Method: Oblimin with Kaiser Normalization.

a. Rotation converged in 25 iterations.

*Structure Matrix*

| | Component | | | |
|---|---|---|---|---|
| | 1 | 2 | 3 | 4 |
| Total Spending in US Dollar | .897 | | | |
| Total Number of Military and Police Deployed | .827 | | | |
| Total Number of Countries Contributing Troops | .819 | | | |
| Number of Civilian Staff | .590 | | | |
| Duration of Peacekeeping Operation in Months | .541 | | | |
| Conflict Issue | .505 | | | |
| Duration of Conflict in Days | | .940 | | |
| Number of Days between Start of Conflict and Start of PKO | | .904 | | |
| Total Number of Fatalities in Conflict | | .548 | | |
| Percentage of Great Powers Involved | | | .860 | |
| Mandate of Peacekeeping Operation | | | .759 | |
| Era of Peacekeeping Operation | | | .735 | |
| Type of Conflict | | | | .799 |
| Region of Peacekeeping Operation | | .539 | | -.591 |

Extraction Method: Principal Component Analysis.

Rotation Method: Oblimin with Kaiser Normalization.

*Component Correlation Matrix*

| Component | 1 | 2 | 3 | 4 |
|-----------|-------|-------|-------|-------|
| 1 | 1.000 | .176 | .100 | .029 |
| 2 | .176 | 1.000 | .031 | .018 |
| 3 | .100 | .031 | 1.000 | .027 |
| 4 | .029 | .018 | .027 | 1.000 |

Extraction Method: Principal Component Analysis.

Rotation Method: Oblimin with Kaiser Normalization.

# Appendix B- Information on Dataset

## File Information

**Notes**

| Output Created | | 21-SEP-2008 18:30:09 |
|---|---|---|
| Comments | | |
| Input | Data | C:\Program Files\SPSS\UNPKO DATASET.sav |
| | Active Dataset | DataSet1 |
| | Filter | <none> |
| | Weight | <none> |
| | Split File | <none> |
| Syntax | | DISPLAY DICTIONARY. |
| Resources | Elapsed Time | 0:00:00.00 |
| | Processor Time | 0:00:00.00 |

[DataSet1] C:\Program Files\SPSS\UNPKO DATASET.sav

# Index

## A

## B

## C

## D

## E

# U

# V

# W

# Y

# About the Authors

Jacques Koko currently serves as Assistant Professor of Conflict Analysis and Dispute Resolution at *Salisbury University* in Maryland. Previously he served as an Adjunct Professor at the Whitehead School of Diplomacy and International Relations at *Seton Hall University* in New Jersey, and as a Senior Political Analyst for *Americans for Informed Democracy*. He also worked as a Senior Social Analyst for the *Institut Africain pour le Développement Economique et Social* (INADES) in Abidjan (Ivory Coast). He holds a Bachelor of Arts degree in Political Philosophy, a Master of Arts in Conflict Transformation and Peacebuilding, and a Ph.D. degree in Conflict Analysis and Resolution, with a focus on the determinants of success in the United Nations peacekeeping operations. Dr. Koko has published articles in both French and English on conflict resolution related issues. He is the author of a book entitled, *National Conference as a Strategy for Conflict Transformation and Peacemaking: The Legacy of the Republic of Benin Model*, published by Adonis & Abbey Publishers (London, UK). His work and research interests encompass organizational conflict and intervention, culture and conflict, peacemaking (all-track diplomacy, negotiation and mediation), peacekeeping, peacebuilding, the national conference and democracy in Africa, the circulation of small weapons in Africa, Somali piracy, and local capacity building.


Essoh Jean Mathieu Claude Essis is a senior public officer and diplomat from the Republic of Côte d'Ivoire (Western Africa). He has a B.A. in Law from the University of Abidjan-Cocody, an M.A. in Public Management from Côte d'Ivoire's National School of Administration, and a Ph.D. in Public policy from George Mason University, Fairfax, Virginia. He was a Fulbright student at GMU (1992-1996) and a Fulbright Visiting Scholar at New York University (2002-2003).

Dr. Essis has held several managerial and diplomatic appointments in the Côte d'Ivoire Civil Service system. He was Sub-Prefect of the rural district of Fronan, Acting Mayor of the suburban municipality of Anyama, Deputy-Secretary of the Ministry of Interior and Decentralization, and Representative of Côte d'Ivoire to the 1995 Review and extension conference of the parties to the nuclear nonproliferation treaty (New York, NY); the 1999 Conference of the International Civil Defense Organization (Beijing, China); and the 1999 Belgium-Côte d'Ivoire Cooperation Commission (Brussels, Belgium).

Between 2002 and 2008, Dr. Essis held several academic positions in the United States, including: Postdoctoral research fellow at the Center on International Cooperation, New York University (August 2002-August 2003); Senior Fellow at the School of Public Policy, George Mason University (October 2003-August 2004); Assistant Professor of Conflict Resolution and Public Policy (August 2004-December 2008) and Interim Chair of the

Department of Conflict Analysis and Resolution (June 2007-February 2008), Graduate School of Humanities and Social Sciences, Nova Southeastern University, Fort Lauderdale, Florida. He was also an Adjunct Professor at NSU's Huizenga School of Business and Entrepreneurship and its Farquhar College of Arts and Sciences.

Dr. Essis has an extensive record of research, teaching and practice on: policy analysis and evaluation, governance and public management; organizational conflict intervention; cross-cultural negotiation and mediation; development and sustainability; as well as African and international affairs.

www.ingramcontent.com/pod-product-compliance
Lightning Source LLC
Chambersburg PA
CBHW021822270326
41932CB00007B/294